MEXICO

ABDO
Publishing Company

MEXICO

by A. M. Buckley

Content Consultant
Allan Burns
Anthropology Department Chair, University of Florida

CREDITS

Published by ABDO Publishing Company, 8000 West 78th Street, Edina, Minnesota 55439. Copyright © 2012 by Abdo Consulting Group, Inc. International copyrights reserved in all countries. No part of this book may be reproduced in any form without written permission from the publisher. The Essential Library™ is a trademark and logo of ABDO Publishing Company.

Printed in the United States of America,
North Mankato, Minnesota
062011
092011

Editor: Melissa York
Copy Editor: Susan M. Freese
Design and production: Emily Love

About the Author: A. M. Buckley is an artist, writer, and children's book author based in Los Angeles, California. Ms. Buckley began her career as a bilingual (English/Spanish) public school teacher in Los Angeles and has been a mentor to many new teachers. She has written several books for children.

Library of Congress Cataloging-in-Publication Data
Buckley, A. M., 1968-
 Mexico / by A.M. Buckley.
    p. cm. -- (Countries of the world)
 Includes bibliographical references and index.
 ISBN 978-1-61783-116-4
 1. Mexico--Juvenile literature. I. Title.
 F1208.5.B83 2011
 972--dc23
                                   2011019672

Cover: Chichén Itzá, Yucatán Peninsula, Mexico

TABLE OF CONTENTS

CHAPTER 1	A Visit to Mexico	6
	Map: Political Boundaries of Mexico	11
	Snapshot	19
CHAPTER 2	Geography: A Rich and Varied Landscape	20
	Map: Geography of Mexico	27
	Map: Climate of Mexico	29
CHAPTER 3	Animals and Nature: Diversity from Land to Sea	33
CHAPTER 4	History: An Epic Past	44
CHAPTER 5	People: A Proud Nation	60
	Map: Population Density of Mexico	63
CHAPTER 6	Culture: Vibrant and Unique	72
CHAPTER 7	Politics: A Tumultuous Democracy	90
CHAPTER 8	Economics: Growing Trade	104
	Map: Resources of Mexico	111
CHAPTER 9	Mexico Today	116
TIMELINE		128
FACTS AT YOUR FINGERTIPS		130
GLOSSARY		134
ADDITIONAL RESOURCES		136
SOURCE NOTES		138
INDEX		142
PHOTO CREDITS		144

CHAPTER 1
A VISIT TO MEXICO

You step from the underground Metro Zócalo and into the enormous plaza at the heart of Mexico City. It's early in the morning, and you're just in time for the first of two daily flag ceremonies, when soldiers of the Mexican Army raise the gigantic national flag over the city square. The order and rigor of the ceremony is impressive, and you enjoy a rare quiet moment in the bustling metropolis as the red, green, and white flag is opened up over the city, fluttering in the warm breeze.

You are standing in the third-largest city square in the world. Officially named the Plaza de la Constitución, locals refer to it as the *Zócalo,* an Italian word that means "pedestal." The name refers to a monument that was planned for the site in the late nineteenth century, shortly after Mexico achieved independence from three centuries of Spanish rule. The monument was never built, but the Zócalo became the thriving center of the city.

Zócalo in Mexico City

ART AND INDEPENDENCE

The National Palace is a treasure trove of art and history. Facing the palace is a bell, the Campana de Dolores. In 1810, the priest Miguel Hidalgo y Costilla rang the bell, sounding the cry for freedom that began the Mexican wars for independence from Spain. Inside the palace, expansive and detailed murals tell the story of Mexico's heritage, culture, and religion. The murals were commissioned by the federal government and created by one of Mexico's most famous artists, Diego Rivera.

To the east is the grand Palacio Nacional, or "National Palace," the seat of the Mexican government. It was built on the same site as the first Aztec palace, the regal throne of one of Mexico's many celebrated and sophisticated pre-Hispanic civilizations. That palace was destroyed and rebuilt by Spanish forces in the sixteenth century, and it has been the seat of the Mexican government since the country's independence.

Opposite the palace, grand hotels, jewelry shops, and even a traditional Mexican hat shop line the Portal de Mercaderes. To the north is the Metropolitan Cathedral, the largest church in Latin America, which was built over the course of three centuries. The offices of the government of Mexico line the south side.

As the flag ceremony winds down, the plaza comes alive with the stamping feet and beating drums of an Aztec dance. Dancers wearing feathered headdresses and shell anklets perform in a circle around the

Aztec dancers in Zócalo, 2007

drummers, engulfed in smoky incense. The dancers chant in Nahuatl, an ancient language native to Mexico.

THE EAGLE AND THE SERPENT

Early in the fourteenth century, the powerful Aztecs traveled through the lake-strewn valley that is now Mexico City in search of a mythical site. Legend has it the Aztecs came upon an eagle atop a cactus devouring a snake. The sight fulfilled a prophecy from the gods, and it was on this site the Aztecs began construction of their main city, Tenochtitlán. The image of the eagle and the snake has survived and forms the central emblem of the Mexican flag. The mythical eagle sits on a white central panel flanked by red and green bands.

The dancers lead the way to the Templo Mayor, an Aztec temple unearthed in 1978. The temple is believed to sit on the exact spot where the Aztecs began their city, Tenochtitlán. As you walk across a central platform where Aztec rulers themselves may have stood, you take some time to admire the historic stone carvings.

From the temple, you make your way through the Centro Histórica, or "Historic Center," a 34-block area surrounding the Zócalo that forms the center of Mexico City. The area is so filled with artistic and historic monuments that it is included on the list of United Nations Educational, Scientific, and Cultural Organization (UNESCO) World Heritage sites—places around the world that are considered so special they are maintained by an international

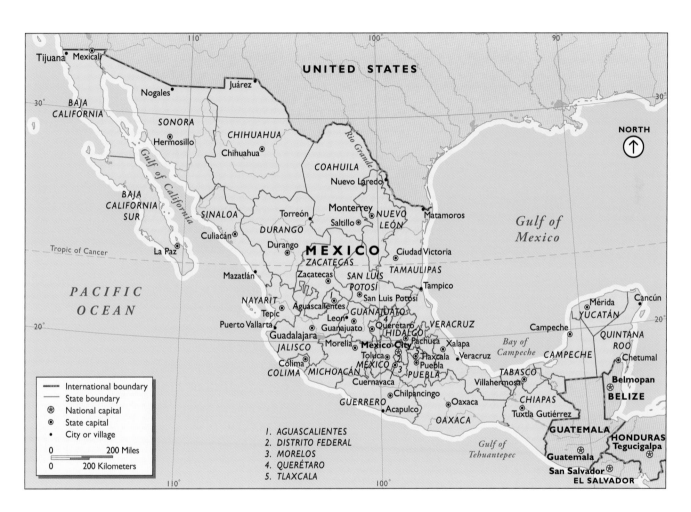

Political Boundaries of Mexico

program. You see many of these sights on your walk, passing museums and churches, office buildings and shops. Along the streets, you see people selling a variety of items, from used books and electronics to woven purses, intricate embroidery, and pots and pans. You even see a man selling cactuses from the back of his truck.

Other street vendors set up food stalls filled with steaming hot tacos, tamales, gorditas, and other snacks. Unable to resist the delicious aromas, you make a stop. As you enjoy a deep-fried corn tortilla filled with beans, cheese, and fresh salsa, you watch the busy street life all around you. Retail clerks scrub the pavement with stiff brushes and soapy pails. Men and women in business suits scurry past vendors hawking services for printing, typing, cleaning, and just about anything else. You pause to admire the lovely ceramic figurines an elderly woman

EL ÁNGEL

Tourists who stroll down the grand Paseo de la Reforma may feel guided from above by an angel. A golden statue of a winged and victorious angel sits atop a 148-foot (45-m) pillar.[1] Considered to be the symbol of Mexico City, the angel was sculpted in 1910 to celebrate 100 years of independence. Its official name is the Monument to Independence, but it is fondly known as El Ángel, or "The Angel."

Mexican craftspeople make and sell beautifully embroidered clothing and other items.

A CITY OF EXTREMES

A walk through Mexico City reveals some of its many diverse neighborhoods. The central metropolitan area of the capital is the Distrito Federal, or "Federal District," which is often referred to by its initials, *DF*. It is divided into 16 boroughs, which are further divided into 1,800 neighborhoods called *colonias*.[2] Beyond DF, Mexico City extends for many miles into a number of crowded suburbs and neighborhoods.

In the city center, north of Chapultepec Park, is Mexico City's wealthy Polanco district, an area made up of seven colonias. Farther on is a breezy and artistic area called Coyoacán, which was the childhood home of Mexican artist Frida Kahlo. The mansions and embassies of Polanco and the colonial homes of Coyoacán are very different from the cinder-block structures with tin or tile roofs that a great many Mexicans call home.

Over the decades, people have continued to migrate to Mexico City to earn a living. As the city filled up, they spread to the outskirts. Many of Mexico City's 19.3 million residents live in the small and often makeshift homes that cover the rolling hillsides outside the city proper.

dressed in traditional Mexican attire has placed on a colorful woven blanket on the sidewalk.

As you wander through town, you make your way to Mexico City's grandest boulevard: the spacious, tree-lined Paseo de la Reforma. Originally built during a brief period of French rule, the street is now the site of numerous construction projects. As you look up, you see cranes and workers building new hotels. On the elegant street, you chance upon a book fair and see a sign for an upcoming art exhibition. To one side lies the *Zona Rosa*—literally, the "Pink Zone"—a bustling center for shopping and nightlife. You make a note to come back in the evening, continuing your stroll to Mexico City's largest park, Bosque de Chapultepec. *Chapultepec* means "grasshopper hill" in Nahuatl.

Entering the park, you cross a vast stretch of greenery dotted with lakes. The park is home to the presidential palace, where the president of Mexico lives, and a handful of world-class museums, including the famous Museo Nacional De Antropología, or "National Anthropological Museum."

You make your way to the expansive city zoo, where animals from all over the world lounge in large, outdoor enclosures. In addition to the two panda bears, you marvel at some of Mexico's rare native animals: the Mexican grey wolf and the exotic xoloitzcuintle, a hairless dog from an ancient Mexican breed.

"May the people and the government respect the rights of all. Between individuals, as between nations, respect for the rights of others is peace."[3]

—*Benito Juárez, president of Mexico from 1861 to 1872*

Before spending the afternoon enjoying art and archaeology in the park's museums, you decide to join locals for a boat ride. Leaning back in the bright blue boat, you listen to the jaunty sound of musicians playing on the shore.

A VIBRANT AND VARIED NATION

In Mexico, it is polite to arrive at someone's house at least 30 minutes late.

Mexico has an epic history that stretches back thousands of years. It was the birthplace of brilliant civilizations and the site of terrible defeats. It has seen its people rise victorious against occupiers only to turn against one another in a long civil war. But through it all, Mexican society has remained proud and indefatigable, creative and resourceful, hardworking and festive.

In the capital, you saw abundant evidence of Mexico's vast history and unique culture. From colonial buildings to stone temples, Gothic churches to contemporary offices, Mexico City is a patchwork of the nation's history. You saw Mexico's vibrant cultural heritage in the faces of the individuals you passed on the streets of Mexico City, where approximately 19.3 million people of varied backgrounds and economic means live and work each day.[4]

Mexico has a long tradition of arts that embraces visual arts, music, dance, and film. From artifacts and sculptures in the capital city's many museums to elaborate murals by famous artists gracing its federal buildings and beautifully made and brightly colored crafts for sale, you saw a range of Mexico's love of and skill in the arts. You could hear it, too, in the array of traditional and contemporary music drifting out from street corners, cantinas, and concert halls.

Dance is only one aspect of Mexico's vibrant culture.

Mexico has grown significantly in recent decades. But despite having the twelfth-largest economy in the world when measured by gross domestic product (GDP), it still faces devastating poverty and a deep divide between the wealthy and the poor.[5] Many of the capital's residents came from villages and towns throughout Mexico. This migration began in the early twentieth century, as Mexicans left close-knit communities in the country to earn a better living in the big city. Millions of people have migrated even farther, making the dangerous journey to find work in the United States, their large northern neighbor.

The sprawling capital of Mexico can be daunting. It is massive, crowded, and smoggy, but it is also dynamic and cosmopolitan. Locals from all walks of life are overwhelmingly resourceful, creative, and welcoming. Mexico is a nation of contrasts, with sleepy villages and teeming cities, but the differences are softened by the strength of Mexicans' shared history and rich culture.

Mexico City is one of the top five most populous cities in the world.

SNAPSHOT

Official name: United Mexican States (In Spanish, Estados Unidos Mexicanos)

Capital city: Mexico City

Form of government: federal republic

Title of leader: president

Currency: peso

Population (July 2011 est.): 113,724,226
World rank: 11

Size: 758,449 square miles (1,964,375 sq km)
World rank: 15

Language: Spanish only, 92.7 percent; Spanish and indigenous languages, 5.7 percent; indigenous only, 0.8 percent; unspecified 0.8 percent

Official religion: none (Unofficial religion: Roman Catholicism, 76.5 percent of population)

Per capita GDP (2010, US dollars): $13,800
World rank: 85

CHAPTER 2

GEOGRAPHY: A RICH AND VARIED LANDSCAPE

Mexico is the fifteenth-largest country in the world. Within its 758,449 square miles (1,964,375 sq km) lie expansive deserts and wet jungles, beautiful beaches and teeming cities with climates that range from temperate to tropical.[1] Mexico is shaped somewhat like an ice-cream cone: wider in the north and narrower in the south. The southern tip curves up to the east, and in the north, a peninsula called Baja California extends into the sea on the western coast. Mexico's territory also includes chains of islands that lie in the Pacific Ocean, Gulf of Mexico, Caribbean Sea, and Gulf of California.

Mexico shares a northern border of 1,952 miles (3,141 km) with the United States and southern borders of 598 miles (962 km) with

Jungle meets sandy shoreline at the Mayan ruins of Tulum.

Guatemala and 155 miles (250 km) with Belize.[2] The Pacific Ocean lies to the west of Mexico, and the Gulf of Mexico lies to the east.

Mexico is divided into 31 states and one federal district: the capital, Mexico City. Mexico City is in the south-central region of the country. It sprawls beyond the city center into many districts and neighborhoods. Other prominent cities include Juárez on the northern border, Guanajuato in the west, and Mérida at the southern tip.

Four mountain ranges cross the country. Two run north to south: the Sierra Madre Occidental along the west and the Sierra Madre Oriental along the east. The majority of Mexico's large cities lie in valleys between these mountains. These two mountain ranges come together at a third range: the Cordillera Neo-Volcánica. It includes

Mexico's highest mountain is a volcano.

MEXICO'S TALLEST PEAKS

Mexico's tallest mountains are among the volcanic mountains in the Cordillera Neo-Volcánica range in central Mexico. These include Pico de Orizaba, which is 18,409 feet (5,611 m) tall, and Iztaccíhuatl, which is 17,126 feet (5,220 m) tall.[3]

Popocatépetl is one of Mexico's many volcanoes.

Mexico's highest mountains and some active volcanoes, including the *Volcán de Fuego*, or "Volcano of Fire."

The fourth mountain range, Sierra Madre del Sur, lies on the Pacific coast in the south of Mexico. It ends at the narrowest part of Mexico, a 137-mile (220-km) strip called the Isthmus of Tehuantepec, in the southern state of Chiapas.[4] On the other side of these mountains is a tropical jungle that extends into Guatemala. To the east, this becomes the tropical forests of the Yucatán Peninsula, the portion of southern Mexico that reaches out and up into a curved tip. This peninsula is bordered on the west by the Gulf of Mexico and by the Caribbean Sea on the east.

The extensive flat area between the mountains that run north to south is the altiplano, or central plain. In the north is the Chihuahuan

A RAIN FOREST BY THE SEA

The Yucatán Peninsula has three distinct ecosystems. The majority of the peninsula is rain forest, a rugged terrain covered in trees and dotted with lagoons, lakes, and waterfalls. The north, west, and east are surrounded by ocean; the white sand beaches are graced with turquoise water and coral reefs just off the coast. In the south, where the peninsula is connected to the rest of Mexico, the Yucatán is composed of a low-lying grassy region made up of a swamp, or tropical savanna.

Sonoran Desert in Baja California

Desert, which extends into the United States. In the south, the central plains are graced with rolling green hills and fertile farmland.

Between the mountains and the seas are narrow coastal plains. These plains are dry on the west coast and include the Sonoran Desert in the northwest. On the east coast, rivers cross the coastal plains. The coasts are home to Mexico's many beaches, which are popular destinations for tourists from all over the world. Among Mexico's many popular beaches are Cabo San Lucas at the tip of the Baja Peninsula, Puerto Vallarta on the western Pacific coast, and Cancún on the northeastern tip of the Yucatán Peninsula.

The Rio Grande is the twentieth-longest river in the world.

The 1,900-mile (3,060-km) Rio Grande begins in the United States and runs along Mexico's northern border before emptying into the Gulf of Mexico.[5] The Lerma River runs through central Mexico and empties into the country's largest freshwater lake, Lake Chapala, which covers 417 square miles (1080 sq km).[6]

HOT AND WET, TEMPERATE AND DRY

Mexico has deserts and tropical beaches, but for the most part, the country has a temperate and relatively warm climate. From May through September, it is hot and humid along the coasts, particularly in the south. From November through February, it can get chilly in the central region of the country.

CHAPTER 3

ANIMALS AND NATURE: DIVERSITY FROM LAND TO SEA

Mexico has the fourth-highest number of species and the second-highest number of distinct ecosystems of any country on the planet.[1] Among the approximately 1,000 species of birds living in Mexico is the national animal, the golden eagle, which represents the country's pride and spirit.[2]

GOLDEN EAGLES

The golden eagle—the largest raptor in North America—is found throughout Mexico, as well as in other parts of North America and as far north as Alaska. Golden eagles typically mate for life and may maintain the same nest for several years in a row. These majestic birds make their nests in high places and protect vast areas of territory from other eagles—sometimes up to 60 square miles (155 sq km). When diving for prey, the golden eagle can reach speeds of 150 miles per hour (240 km/h).

The golden eagle, Mexico's national animal, is one of many species of birds that live in the country.

Dolphin pods often gather in the Sea of Cortez.

THE ANIMALS OF MEXICO

Mexico has an astonishing level of biodiversity, as it is home to 10 to 12 percent of the world's many plants and animals. In addition, Mexico is home to a staggering 83 percent of the world's known insect species, as well as many unidentified species, scientists believe. Mexico also has 530 species of mammals, or approximately 10 percent of the world's total, and more than 11 percent of the world's bird species.[3]

A wide variety of water animals—such as whales, sea lions, sea turtles, seals, and dolphins—live in Mexican oceans. And on land, mammals including wolves, deer, coyotes, and bobcats live in the mountains of northern Mexico. The nation's forests, particularly the tropical forests in the southeast, provide homes for five species of big cats—pumas, jaguars, jaguarundis, margays, and ocelots—as well as spider and howler monkeys and tapirs. Among Mexico's numerous reptiles are many species of lizards, alligators, crocodiles, turtles, and snakes.

Mexico also has an extensive and varied bird population. Water birds include pelicans, ducks, and storks, and raptors include the golden eagle. In addition to hummingbirds and songbirds, Mexico has a variety of exotic birds, such as macaws, toucans, and quetzal, which live in the southeastern jungles.

GIANT CACTUSES AND TROPICAL TREES

With at least 26,000 different species of flora, Mexico has the fourth-most-diverse plant life in the world.[4] The warm and humid weather and varied regions allow different kinds of plants to thrive

THE PLIGHT OF THE VAQUITA

A number of Mexico's many animals are endemic, or native, to the region and do not live anywhere else in the world. One of the nation's endemic animals is a small harbor porpoise called the vaquita. It is one of the world's most critically endangered cetacean, a group of marine mammals that includes porpoises, dolphins, and whales.[5]

The vaquita lives in the Sea of Cortez, also called the Gulf of California, which is the body of water between Baja California and the main territory of Mexico. The vaquita has a stocky body and rounded nose, and its tail resembles that of a dolphin. The vaquita is grey in color with distinct markings around its eyes and mouth; its belly is lighter gray or white.

Vaquitas are becoming increasingly rare. The most accurate recent count, in 1997, estimated 567 animals, and that number is assumed to be decreasing.[6] Fishing poses the primary threat to this marine animal. Although fisheries do not try to catch vaquitas, the porpoises sometimes get tangled in fishing nets and die. The Mexican government and world wildlife foundations are trying to protect vaquitas in a number of ways, including publicizing their plight and trying to persuade fisheries to use other methods or to avoid the Sea of Cortez.

QUIRKY PLANTS

One of Mexico's many unusual plants is the boojum tree, which resembles a dusky green upside-down carrot. Boojum trees grow in central Baja California and in the Chihuahuan Desert and reach up to 50 feet (15 m) in height.

around Mexico—everything from desert cactuses to the deciduous trees of the expansive temperate forests to the lush plants of the tropical jungles. Among these are many plants that have been cultivated over the centuries for food, including corn, tomatoes, avocados, and cactuses.

A large variety of desert plants thrive in the northern and western plains of the Chihuahuan and Sonoran Deserts. These are two of the most biologically diverse deserts in the world and are home to more than 400 cactus species.[7] Baja California is home to the world's tallest cactus, the cardón, which has been known to grow up to 65 feet (20 m) tall.

Mexico is so diverse because it is home to both North and South American species.

Mexico has the twelfth-largest area covered by forest of any country.[8] In the mountains, the pine forests include half the world's total species of pine, and approximately 135 species of oak grow at lower altitudes.[9] At higher elevations in the south of Mexico, the forests are covered in clouds, earning them the nickname "cloud forests." Evergreen forests thrive in the

Cardón cactuses in Baja California

SELVA LACANDONA

The biggest tropical forest in Mexico is the Selva Lacandona, or Lacandon Jungle, which lies on the east side of the southern state of Chiapas. Even though this jungle is small compared to the entire country of Mexico, it contains a huge number of plants and animals, including nearly half the total species of butterflies in Mexico. Unfortunately, the size of the jungle is shrinking due to farming, cattle ranching, and other environmental threats. Even so, it remains a place of natural beauty, filled with misty peaks, placid lakes, tumbling waterfalls, and thick green foliage dotted with the bright colors of butterflies and exotic birds.

humid southeastern region and in the rain forests in the southwestern region. An abundance of wildflowers and air plants—plants that grow on trees—can be found in Mexico's forests as well.

BIODIVERSITY UNDER THREAT

Mexico faces environmental threats similar to other industrialized nations, including growing deserts, urban sprawl, and pollution. Mexico also faces a serious water shortage. As a result, approximately 10 percent of Mexicans do not have a water supply in their homes. Millions more lack a drainage system, so they have water but it is not fit for drinking.[10] The country has had severe droughts, including one as recently as 2007, and it has ongoing problems bringing the water supply from the humid south to the drier but more populous north.

Loggers, hunters, and poachers pose additional threats to Mexico's environment. Despite protection, the nation's forests continue to be cut and its rare animals hunted. The Mexican government struggles to enforce its strict policies against aggressive loggers.

Although Mexico has ongoing environmental problems, the nation's government has taken strong steps to conserve and protect the landscape. At least 13 percent of Mexico's territory is under some form of local, state, or federal protection, including 67 national parks and 53 biosphere reserves.[11] Those created early in the twentieth century tend to be small, but more recent parks are larger and protect regions including fragile coastlines, coral reefs, and a variety of forests. The biosphere reserves aim to keep designated ecosystems safe from interference and are administered by the Mexican government and UNESCO. These reserves encourage sustainable use of the local natural resources and offer protection for the environment and the animals living there.

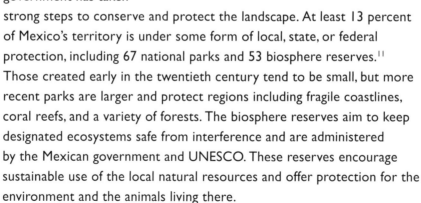

THE BUTTERFLIES OF MICHOACÁN

Every year, hundreds of thousands of monarch butterflies make their way south from Canada across North America to Mexico. A great many of them arrive in the town of Angangueo in Michoacán, where they are protected in a federal sanctuary. The tremendous number of beautiful orange and black butterflies covers the trees and fills the sky.

Cuatro Ciénegas are protected marshes in the
Mexican state of Coahuila.

Despite strict conservation laws, Mexico has not always been able to protect the environment or those who try to aid it. For example, in 2007, a man was murdered while gathering information on illegal logging for Greenpeace, an international conservation group. Similar incidents of violence against people trying to curb logging or hunting have been reported.

Even so, the Mexican government continues to strive to protect and conserve the environment. It has pledged zero tolerance for illegal logging and promotes renewable energy. Among the general population, environmental concerns are on the rise. Mexico's largest environmental group is Pronatura.

ENDANGERED SPECIES

Because of environmental threats and damage to natural habitats, a great many of Mexico's animals are vulnerable to extinction. According to the International Union for Conservation of Nature (IUCN) Red List, 688 species of land, water, and amphibious animals were in danger of extinction in 2007.[12] Some endangered species included the jaguar, the ocelot, the southern tamandua (anteater), the sea otter, and the green macaw, along with four kinds of parrots, seven kinds of sea turtles, and many more animals.

Mexico has 30 extinct, 190 critically endangered, and 234 endangered species.

Among the many animals facing extinction, the ridley sea turtle has become a success story. This turtle, which lives primarily in the Gulf of

ENDANGERED SPECIES IN MEXICO

According to the International Union for Conservation of Nature (IUCN), Mexico is home to the following numbers of species that are categorized by the organization as Critically Endangered, Endangered, or Vulnerable:

Mammals	99
Birds	55
Reptiles	94
Amphibians	211
Fishes	150
Mollusks	5
Other Invertebrates	74
Plants	255
Total	943[13]

Mexico and parts of the southern United States, was facing extinction when the Mexican and US governments initiated a large-scale operation to save it. The relief effort began in Mexico, where the government passed laws banning the harvesting of the turtle and initiated extensive efforts to protect and support its fragile nests. The effort was supported by US laws. The two nations have had a powerful effect in replenishing the population of ridley sea turtles.

Jaguars are in danger of extinction.

CHAPTER 4

HISTORY: AN EPIC PAST

The first people to arrive in North America and Mexico crossed a land bridge from Asia, possibly as early as 30,000 years ago. Archaeological evidence indicates that they lived as hunters and gatherers in the area that is today Mexico from approximately 12,000 to 8,000 BCE. At first, they hunted the wild animal herds roaming the valleys. Eventually, they began to cultivate indigenous plants, including beans, corn, and squash. Villages based on agriculture were established during 7000 to 3000 BCE.

The villages grew into cities, which developed into the vast empires of highly sophisticated civilizations. For approximately 3,000 years, some of the most fascinating civilizations in the ancient world thrived in the area that is now Mexico. Archaeologists use the term *Mesoamerica* to refer to the region where these civilizations existed, which included

The people of the early Mesoamerican Olmec culture carved giant heads out of stone.

central, southern, and eastern Mexico, as well as parts of Guatemala, Belize, and Honduras.

The first of these civilizations, known as the Olmec, existed from 1200 to 400 BCE along the humid southeastern coast of Mexico, in what are now the states of Veracruz and Tabasco. This advanced society developed writing, a compass, a calendar, and advanced works of art. Giant stone heads carved by the Olmec are some of the most unique artworks from the ancient world. The Olmec religion and its deities, especially a feathered serpent god, influenced culture in the region for centuries.

OLMEC HEADS

The Olmec carved a number of giant stone heads, many of which stand taller than a human. Each head is unique and wears what appears to be a helmet. Archaeologists believe the Olmec carved each head from a single boulder of volcanic rock. Scholars speculate that the heads were created as portraits of warriors or kings.

THE GOLDEN AGE OF MEXICO

The time period from approximately 200 BCE to 900 CE has been called the Golden Age of Mexico. Numerous advanced civilizations thrived in the area during this time.

The Pyramid of the Sun in Teotihuacán is one of the largest structures of its kind in the Western Hemisphere.

At the beginning of the first century CE, a massive city called Teotihuacán was built in central Mexico. Archaeologists are uncertain which Mesoamerican culture built the city, but it was constructed in a valley in central Mexico, not far from the area that is now Mexico City. The city was laid out in a massive grid plan, similar to many modern cities, and included two pyramids, the Pyramid of the Sun and the Pyramid of the Moon. The city was the center of a vast empire.

MAYAN INVENTIONS

Because several Mesoamerican civilizations existed in the same area—some during the same time period—they had a strong influence on one another and shared many features. For example, the Olmec are believed to have invented the calendar and the concept of zero. However, the Maya extended these ideas, developing an even more sophisticated calendar and a counting system based on blocks of 20.

The Mayan writing system is believed to be the most advanced of any among the Mesoamerican societies. It consisted of phonetic symbols such as letters, other symbols that referred to syllables, and logograms, which are pictures or symbols that represent entire words or concepts. Thousands of Mayan scripts have been discovered, most of them inscribed or carved into stone, wooden slabs, or ceramic pottery. The Maya also wrote on bark, applying ink with a quill or brush and binding the bark in book-like forms called codex.

In Mayan society, writing was valued and scribes were highly regarded. Examples of Mayan artwork often picture people of the noble or ruling classes with inkpots or brushes, indicating their roles as scribes.

Around the same time, the Mayan civilization began developing. Considered by many archaeologists to be Mexico's most advanced ancient civilization, the Maya flourished in the Yucatán Peninsula, southwestern Mexico, and parts of Guatemala, Honduras, El Salvador, and Belize during the years 250 to 900. The Maya were a sophisticated society, with complex city-states filled with advanced architectural monuments. Many of their pyramids and palaces remain standing today. In addition, the Maya developed a more sophisticated calendar than anything that had existed before, used a complex written language, and made discoveries in astronomy and mathematics, including the invention of the number zero.

Mayan society was not able to sustain large cities, so much of the civilization collapsed near the end of the eighth century. Drought led to infighting among the Maya and a shortage of food, which forced the people to leave their cities between 900 and 1000 CE. They continued living in smaller villages, however, and their descendants still do up to this day.

Other ancient civilizations in Mexico included the Toltec, which flourished between 700 and 1200, the Zapotec, the Tarascos, and the last of the great Mesoamerican empires, the Aztecs. The Aztecs, also known as the Mexica, were a nomadic people until their priests led them to the central valley of Mexico, where they settled in approximately 1325. There, the Aztecs constructed their primary city, Tenochtitlán, where Mexico City stands today.

The Aztecs were great warriors, and they soon formed an alliance with two other states in the

CENTER OF THE UNIVERSE

The Aztecs constructed hundreds of temple complexes in their main city of Tenochtitlán. One of them, the Templo Mayor, still remains near the main square in Mexico City. It was dedicated to the hummingbird god, Huitzilopochtli, and rain god, Tlátoc. The Aztecs considered this place to be the center of the universe.

The Aztecs and the Maya were the first people to consume chocolate.

valley. Together, they controlled most of Mexico in an empire composed of 38 provinces and approximately 5 million people.[1] Aztec society was very religious and highly stratified, or class based, with the priests and nobles receiving the best treatment and the serfs or slaves living difficult lives at the bottom of society. The Aztecs improved farming techniques using only stone and wood tools. They also built elaborate temple complexes for their many religious rituals and ceremonies, which included human sacrifice to the gods. They demanded taxes and tribute from all of the people they ruled.

THE SPANISH CONQUEST

The arrival of the first Europeans in Mexico had disastrous consequences for the native peoples. In 1519, a Spanish expedition of 11 ships and approximately 700 men led by Hernán Cortés arrived in Mexico from Cuba.[2] The ships landed in eastern Mexico, near what is now Veracruz. Upon seeing the Spaniards on horses—animals previously unknown in Mesoamerica—a great many people fled in terror. However, as the Spanish continued their journey inland, some of the Aztecs' enemies joined the expedition.

A native drawing depicts the violence that occurred between Hernán Cortés and the Aztecs.

When the Aztec emperor Montezuma learned of the strangers' arrival, he believed they could fulfill an Aztec legend. Montezuma believed the god Quetzalcóatl would arrive in the area that same year. Still uncertain whether the newcomers were invaders or the representation of a god, the Aztec emperor did not raise troops in battle but invited the explorers into the city and hosted them in grand fashion.

Founded in 1551, the University of Mexico was one of the first universities in the New World.

The Spaniards stayed for several months but eventually attacked, killing approximately 200 Aztec noblemen. The Spaniards fled when they were outnumbered but soon returned with reinforcements. Some 100,000 members of other tribes, displeased with the ruling Aztecs, joined the newcomers in battle.[3] While the Spaniards regrouped, an epidemic of smallpox broke out in the city of Tenochtitlán. Brought to Mexico by the Spaniards, the disease killed much of the indigenous population, including the emperor.

In May 1521, the Spanish entered the city again, and within three weeks, they took control. They ruled New Spain in a class-based society that placed Spanish people, known as criollos, at the top and the indigenous peoples below them. Spanish priests and missionaries helped government officials settle the indigenous tribes into Spanish towns and cities. The Spanish mined silver, gold, and other natural resources from Mexico's rich terrain, sending treasure back to their king in Spain and growing rich on the rest of their findings.

This colonial society persisted for almost 300 years. However, the native population grew more and more discontented at their treatment by the colonizers.

MEXICAN INDEPENDENCE

On September 16, 1810, a priest named Miguel Hidalgo y Costilla launched the Mexican wars for independence in the town of Dolores in Guanajuato. For nearly 11 years, the discontented indigenous population rebelled against the Spaniards. They won their freedom in 1821. A short-lived Mexican Empire was established under Emperor Agustín de Iturbide, but he was removed from office within two years. The republic of Mexico, officially the United Mexican States, was established with the constitution of 1824. Political factions disagreed about how much power the central government should have and argued over whether Catholicism should be the country's official religion.

MEXICO'S FIRST PRESIDENT

Guadalupe Victoria was the first president of the United Mexican States. Born in 1786 in Tamazuela, Mexico, Victoria was originally named Manuel Félix Fernández. He was a law student at the start of the Mexican wars for independence, but he soon left school to join the fight. The Virgin of Guadalupe, a popular religious figure in Mexico, was the symbol of independence, and the young militant changed his name to reflect his dedication to the cause of freedom. Victoria joined the revolt against the first emperor in 1823 and was elected Mexico's first president in 1824.

SANTA ANNA

On March 6, 1836, Antonio López de Santa Anna, a popular political leader and general, led Mexican forces to a victory against the United States at the Battle of the Alamo in Texas. However, the Mexicans eventually lost the Mexican-American War. Santa Anna served several terms as Mexico's president and spent time in exile in the United States. A controversial figure in Mexican history, he is remembered variously as a hero of Mexican independence and as the general who led Mexico into military defeat against the United States.

From Mexico's earliest days as an independent nation, it endured complex relations with its neighbor to the north, the United States. In 1836, the people of Texas— then part of Mexico—declared their independence. This set off a territorial battle that led to the Mexican-American War, which lasted from 1846 to 1848. At the end of the bloody war, Mexico was forced to allow Texas to join the United States and to give its territory north of the Rio Grande to the United States, which included the modern-day US states of California, Nevada, Utah, and parts of New Mexico, Colorado, and Arizona.

At the end of the war a group of intellectuals, including the Zapotec lawyer and political leader Benito Juárez, met to draft a plan to reform the nation's government. This led to a new constitution in 1857, which formally abolished slavery, established secular public education, and curtailed the powers of the Catholic Church. In 1861, the Mexican people cheered the election of the first president descended from the

In 2010, members of the Mexican Army reenacted battles from the Mexican-American War, which began in 1846.

indigenous people, Benito Juárez, who remains a national hero in Mexico today.

Before long, the young nation was disturbed by yet another European invasion. French forces controlled Mexico City from 1863 to 1867. The occupation ended when Mexicans executed the French-appointed emperor Maximilian. Porfirio Díaz, a general during the French intervention, emerged as Mexico's president. Winning five consecutive reelections, Díaz ruled from 1876 to 1911, the head of a stable but oppressive government known as the Porfiriato.

In 1910, a new candidate named Francisco Madero seemed likely to beat Díaz in the presidential election. However, he was jailed, apparently to remove him from competition. He called for revolt against Díaz, and the people rose up and overthrew the president in May 1911. The revolutionaries did not agree on a new direction for the country, however, and it fell into a devastating civil war known as the Mexican Revolution. By the end of the war, approximately one in eight Mexicans had been killed.[4] In 1920, President Álvaro Obregón took office and began reconstructing Mexico, instituting reforms, building schools, and redistributing land to the poor.

LEADERS OF THE REVOLUTION

The Mexican Revolution saw the rise of two Mexican heroes: Emiliano Zapata and Pancho Villa. Zapata was a radical leader from the state of Morelos whose famous cry, "Tierra y libertad," or "Land and freedom," symbolized his call for land to be returned from the wealthy to the poor. He energized rural Mexicans. The man known as Pancho Villa was born in the northern state of Durango. Initially behaving as a Robin Hood–like bandit and fighting for the rights of the poor on both sides of the US-Mexican border, Villa later emerged as a heroic leader of the Mexican Revolution.

Pancho Villa was a rebel leader during the Mexican Revolution.

The next president, Plutarco Elías Calles, founded the Partido Revolucionario Nacional, or the "National Revolutionary Party," in 1929. Now called the Partido Revolucionario Institucional (PRI), or

"Institutional Revolutionary Party," Calles's party remained in control of the Mexican government for much of the twentieth century. During this time, Mexico advanced economically and socially, and its capital, Mexico City, developed into one of the world's most cosmopolitan cities. In addition, hundreds of thousands of peasants and small farmers received land from the government.

Although the PRI was widely supported at first, it faced increasing criticism and charges of election fraud from the 1960s onward. The situation worsened dramatically in October 1968, when hundreds of student protestors were killed in Mexico City after government forces stepped in to stop the protest.

Before he was president, Vicente Fox worked for Coca-Cola.

During the latter half of the twentieth century, Mexico experienced swings in economic growth. The nation depended in large part on the sale of oil, managed by the national company, Pemex. The Mexican economy rose and fell with oil prices throughout the 1970s and 1980s. A huge growth in population made Mexico's economic challenges more difficult. The gap between the rich and the poor remained large and unemployment was an ongoing challenge, yet the middle class began growing.

Eighty years of one-party rule ended in 2000 with the election of Vicente Fox of the Partido Acción Nacional (PAN), or the "National Action Party." PAN stayed in power after the 2006 election, when Felipe Calderón won the presidency. Along with swings in economic fortunes

Vicente Fox campaigning for president, July 1999

and high unemployment, Mexico has struggled with gang violence from drug dealers. Calderón has made fighting these gangs a cornerstone of his presidency.

CHAPTER 5

PEOPLE: A PROUD NATION

Because Mexico was occupied by Spain for three centuries, many Mexicans are a mix of Spanish and Amerindian ancestry. The Mexican culture integrates aspects of native customs, language, and religion with European ideas. Creativity, ingenuity, and artistry tend to be part of Mexican heritage. Mexicans also tend to value family and community and to take pride in their culture—a culture that blends Amerindian, African, and European elements in a way that is unique throughout the world.

A majority of Mexicans—60 percent—are a combination of Amerindian, Spanish, and sometimes African ancestry, an ethnicity called mestizo. Thirty percent are Amerindian or predominantly Amerindian, an ethnicity called *indígenas*, or indigenous, and 9 percent are white or of mostly European ancestry.[1]

Native customs are easily seen throughout many parts of Mexico.

LARGEST GROUPS OF INDIGENOUS PEOPLES IN MEXICO

Indigenous Group	Approximate Number Living in Mexico	Region Located
Nahau (descendents of Aztecs)	2 million	Central Mexico
Yucatec Maya (descendents of the Maya)	1.5 million	Yucatán Peninsula
Tzotziles	400,000	Chiapas
Tzeltales	500,000	Chiapas
Zapotec	800,000	Oaxaca
Mixtec	700,000	Oaxaca, Guerrero, and Puebla
Totonacs	400,000	Veracruz and Puebla
Purépecha	200,000	Michoacán[2]

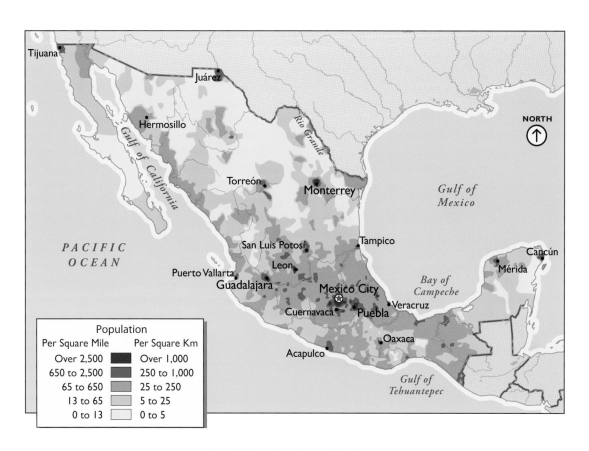

Population Density of Mexico

In addition, a number of people from other countries live in Mexico, making it a multicultural nation. Among these people are many from the United States and Canada.

YOU SAY IT!

English	Spanish
Hello	Hola (OH-lah)
How are you?	¿Cómo está usted? [formal] (KOH-moh ehs-TAH OO-stehd) ¿Cómo estás? [informal] (KOH-moh ehs-TAHS)
What's your name?	¿Cómo te llamas? (KOH-moh tay YAH-mahs)
Good-bye	Adiós (ah-dee-OHS)
Good morning	Buenos días (BWAY-nohs DEE-ahs)
Good night	Buenas noches (BWAY-nahs NOH-chehss)
Thank you	Gracias (GRAH-see-ahs)
You're welcome	De nada (day nah-dah)

A significant number of people come to Mexico from Central and South America, many seeking refuge from unstable political situations in their own countries. People from China, Japan, Korea, and the Philippines, as well as parts of Africa and the Middle East, also live in Mexico.

Mexico has a population of more than 100 million, and the vast majority of its people speak Spanish. This makes Mexico the most populous Spanish-speaking country in the world.[3] There is no official language of Mexico, but 92.7 percent of Mexican people speak Spanish and another 5.7 percent speak Spanish in addition to one of Mexico's native languages. In total, more than 98 percent of the population speaks Spanish.[4]

A small number of Mexicans (0.8 percent) speak only an indigenous language.[5] Approximately 60 of these regional Amerindian languages are still spoken today, including Mayan and Nahuatl. Linguists have identified 139 more languages that are no longer spoken.[6] Since each language signifies a specific native culture, the disappearance of these languages means that more than 100 native cultures have vanished from Mexico.

In 2003, the Mexican government passed the Law of Linguistic Rights, granting official designation to indigenous languages. As a result, millions of Mexican schoolchildren now receive bilingual education in Spanish and their local language.

Spanish is spoken by at least 358 million people worldwide; more than 100 million live in Mexico.

Since the 1970s, more and more Mexicans have migrated to the nation's cities. Today, the population is increasingly urban, with **78** percent living in cities or urban centers and the rest living in rural villages.[7] The average life expectancy in Mexico is 76.47 years, the seventy-third highest among nations in the world.[8]

A ROMAN CATHOLIC COUNTRY

When the Spanish conquistadores came to Mexico, they brought guns and horses as well as the Roman Catholic religion. The Spanish colonized Mexico, overtaking the native Aztec civilization, and they ruled for three centuries before Mexicans won their independence. But Mexicans embraced the imported religion,

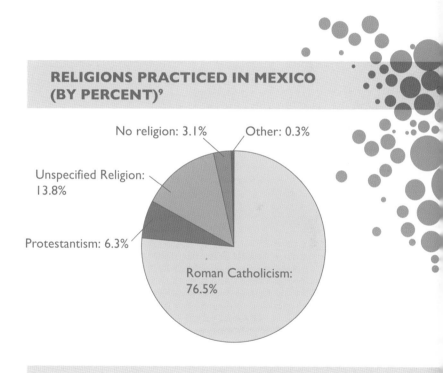

RELIGIONS PRACTICED IN MEXICO (BY PERCENT)[9]

No religion: 3.1%
Other: 0.3%
Unspecified Religion: 13.8%
Protestantism: 6.3%
Roman Catholicism: 76.5%

Mexico City is home to more than 19 million people.

An altar for Our Lady of Guadalupe, the patron saint of Mexico, stands on a street corner in Mexico City.

integrating native customs into Catholicism and adopting it on a wide scale. Today, Mexico has the second-largest Catholic population in the world.[10]

Mexico does not have an official religion, but three in four Mexicans are Roman Catholic, making it the country's primary religion. When the

Spanish brought Catholicism to Mexico, they adapted to local customs, celebrating religious holidays much as the locals had always done but moving the dates to those considered holy by Catholics. The transition to Catholicism was further aided in 1531, when an Aztec potter named Juan Diego was reported to have had an encounter with Jesus's mother, Mary, in which she looked like a Mexican woman. Mexicans embraced this image, and Nuestra Señora de Guadalupe, the Virgin Mary of Guadalupe, became the unofficial patron saint of Mexico.

Despite the heavy influence of Catholicism, indigenous beliefs and religious practices continue to influence Mexican culture and spirituality. Indigenous belief in spirits that are part of the natural world survived in *curanderos*, or traditional healers. They call on both saints and spirits as they use natural cures, such as herbs and plants. Mexicans in general tend to be interested in the supernatural and to focus on the importance of coincidence, which is reminiscent of pre-Hispanic spiritual beliefs.

Today, more and more Mexicans are joining other religious denominations, including the Church of the Latter Day Saints (Mormons), Presbyterian churches, and Evangelical churches.

MEXICANS ABROAD

Mexico is home to a large, multinational population, but at the same time, approximately one in seven Mexicans leaves the country to work in the United States at some

It is not uncommon to see public displays of religion such as altars on the street.

CHANGING VILLAGES

Mexicans have been migrating to the United States since at least the 1980s, when a deep recession sent many Mexicans north to find work. This migration has changed village communities throughout Mexico and has had deep social, cultural, and economic impacts on Mexican families and lifestyles. The town of Tendeparacua in Michoacán provides a dramatic example. In 1985, it reportedly had 6,000 residents, but by 2006, it had only 600.[12]

As men have left to seek work in the North, some villages have been left with a tiny population of working-age men. In recent decades, more women have left, too, sometimes leaving behind young children to be raised by their grandparents.

The trip north is very dangerous, and many Mexicans die en route each year. Some die from starvation or dehydration, and others are abandoned in the desert by corrupt coyotes, people paid to guide immigrants to the United States. Still others die in violence along the border. Yet millions of Mexicans do make it safely to the United States, and after finding work, they are able to send home large amounts of money.

point in their life.[11] In some areas of the United States that used to belong to Mexico—such as Arizona, California, New Mexico, and Texas—families have long histories that include relatives living on both sides of the border.

Even as Mexicans continue to migrate to the United States, their ties to home and family remain strong. Mexicans working outside their hometowns or local villages typically send large amounts of money back to their families. In fact, compared to migrant workers worldwide, Mexicans send home some of the largest amounts. Having this support has improved life for many families in Mexico, allowing for the construction of new

Migrant worker Daniel Roblero looks for work in Florida so he can send money to his family in Mexico.

homes and infrastructure. However, it has also taken a toll on families and communities as migrants are not home to fill local jobs or help raise their children.

CHAPTER 6
CULTURE: VIBRANT AND UNIQUE

Mexico is well known for its delicious and unique cuisine, colorful fiestas, and dramatic indigenous dances. Art, music, dance, architecture, and literature have been important parts of Mexican life and culture for centuries.

Holidays and festivals throughout the country tend to revolve around religious events. Holidays include Semana Santa, or "Holy Week," which is the week before Easter. On November 2, Mexicans celebrate Día de los Muertos, or the "Day of the Dead," honoring family members who have passed away. One of the most important holidays in Mexico is Día de Nuestra Señora de Guadalupe, the celebration of the Virgin of Guadalupe, held on December 12. People from all over the country make pilgrimages—many riding long distances on bicycles—to visit the patron saint's church in Mexico City, the Basilica of Guadalupe.

Toys, candies, and bread are made into skulls, and skulls and skeletons also decorate displays for the Day of the Dead.

PIÑATAS

Many Mexican festivals, including the Christmas celebration, include a game that revolves around the piñata, a hollow container decorated with paper and filled with candies or other treats. Blindfolded players whack the suspended piñata with a stick, hoping to break the paper or clay form and release a cascade of treats.

The piñata is an example of Mexican culture's roots in both indigenous and European traditions. A similar game originated in both Europe and Mesoamerica. The Maya had a game in which blindfolded players hit at a suspended clay pot. Aztec priests placed a clay pot decorated with feathers and filled with treats in front of an image of the god Huitzilopochtli; when the pot broke, the treats fell at the feet of the god. Explorer Marco Polo is said to have brought a similar tradition from China to Europe, where it developed during the fourteenth century. The Spaniards later brought the tradition to Mexico, where it resonated with familiar indigenous games and developed into the current pastime.

December 12 also starts the Christmas season in Mexico, an important time in this predominantly Catholic country. On December 24, Mexico celebrates Nochebuena, or "Holy Night," and the next day, Christmas, commemorates the birth of Jesus Christ. For nine days leading up to December 24, Mexicans hold processions called *posadas*. Participants walk from one house to another, singing songs and imitating the holy family as they searched for lodging for the birth of their son in biblical times. During the Christmas season, people take time off from work to be with family and friends and to take part in community events.

FOOD AND DRINK

Mexican food—famous for tacos, burritos, and quesadillas—is richly diverse. Plants cultivated in the region thousands of years ago remain important to Mexican cuisine today, including avocados, tomatoes, and maize, or corn. The main ingredients of most Mexican foods are corn, beans, squash, and a variety of dry or fresh chilies, which are also indigenous to the region. A range of vegetables makes for colorful dishes.

Mexican dishes are often served on or with corn tortillas, although people in the northern states of Mexico eat flour tortillas. Parts of the cactuses that grow in the deserts are also used in many dishes, including nopalitos, or cactus salad. Seafood, including lobster and shrimp, is often served grilled. Meats include chicken, pork, beef, and others. Spices that contribute to the unique flavors of Mexican food are cinnamon, clove, red achiote, and cumin. Popular herbs include thyme and oregano, plus plenty of cilantro.

One of the most popular and unique Mexican dishes is mole, a complex sauce made with chocolate, nuts, chilies, and spices that can be served over chicken, turkey, or pork. A popular dish from Puebla is *chiles en nogada*, which is stuffed chilies covered in walnut cream sauce and sprinkled with pomegranates. *Machaca* is a kind of spiced, shredded beef from Monterrey. *Tlayudas*, which come from Oaxaca, are made from big tortillas covered in beans,

POPULAR DRINKS

Fresh fruit juices sold at stalls called *juguerías* are popular among Mexicans, as are a type of shake called *licuado*, made with milk, honey, bananas, and other fruits. Also popular are *aguas frescas*, or "fresh waters," drinks similar to iced tea that contain water embellished with herbs or plants and fruits such as cantaloupe blended with plain water. Coffee, hot chocolate, and corn-based drinks are also common.

The most famous alcoholic drink in Mexico is tequila, made from the blue agave cactus that grows well in the state of Jalisco in southern Mexico. Real tequila can only be produced in this region. A regulatory council ensures that liquor made elsewhere is not called tequila.

cheese, and various toppings. In Yucatán, the favorite snack is the *panucho*, a deep-fried tortilla stuffed with refried beans and covered with chicken and avocado.

A staple of Mexican food is a group of dishes called *antojitos*. The word *antojito* translates into English as "whim" or "craving." This category embraces a range of popular Mexican dishes, including tacos, enchiladas, tostadas, quesadillas, chilaquiles, tamales, and sopes. All are made with the base of a corn tortilla or corn meal and include delicious toppings such as cheese, beans, vegetables, and meat. For example, enchiladas are stuffed tortillas covered in sauce and baked, whereas tostadas are fried tortillas filled with various toppings.

In Mexico, it is polite to leave a little food on your plate at the end of a meal.

SPORTS AND GAMES

By far the most popular sport in Mexico is *futból*, or soccer. Mexican soccer teams have been in the international World Cup tournament 14 times and are considered to provide tough competition worldwide. In Mexico, matches with teams from all over the country attract large crowds, and millions more watch matches on TV. The two most popular teams are the Eagles, also called Mexico City, and the Chivas, or Goats, of Guadalajara. Mexico hosted the World Cup in 1970 and 1986.

Other popular sports in Mexico include bullfighting, wrestling, and rodeo. Mexico City has the largest bullfighting ring in the world,

La Monumental. Because the country does not have an age limit for matadors, or bullfighters, children as young as ten take on bulls in some fights. However, in recent years, animal rights activists have led a rising movement to stop the practice of bullfighting altogether. Wrestling in Mexico is known as *lucha libre*, and it is as much a spectacle as a sport. Masked wrestlers—one clad in white and the other in black—compete in a fight symbolic of good against evil in which the good guy always wins. A sport similar to rodeo called *charrería* includes competitions on horseback and other events. Rodeo in the United States originated in Mexico.

Mexico also has national baseball and basketball leagues and a college football league. Fishing is popular as well, particularly in Baja California and on the Pacific coast, and various water sports including surfing are becoming more common. Mexico City hosted the Summer Olympic Games in 1968, the first Latin American city to host this large international competition.

MEXICAN ART

Mexico has a long and well-known tradition of painting, drawing, and sculpture. It embraces some of the world's most refined examples of ancient art, such as Olmec carved heads, Mayan architecture, and Aztec carvings. The nation has also been home to several of the twentieth

Soccer fans standing in the Zócalo cheer enthusiastically during the match between Mexico and France at the 2010 World Cup.

DIEGO AND FRIDA

No two Mexican artists have captured the world's hearts and attention like Diego Rivera, born on December 8, 1886, in Guanajuato, Mexico, and Frida Kahlo, born on July 6, 1907. Rivera married Kahlo when she was 22 years old. At the time, Rivera was already a famous muralist and painter, but Kahlo had only recently begun to paint. She was recuperating from a terrible streetcar accident that had been followed by numerous operations. The couple survived a stormy but committed relationship that included divorce, remarriage, and numerous affairs.

Rivera studied art in Mexico and Europe, and his numerous murals and paintings explore Mexican culture, history, politics, and heroes. Although Kahlo was similarly inspired by her country, particularly its indigenous past, her more intimate paintings symbolically depict her physical and emotional suffering.

century's most renowned artists, including Diego Rivera, Rufino Tamayo, David Alfaro Siqueiros, and Frida Kahlo.

Mexican artists are particularly known for a tradition of magnificent murals depicting political, cultural, and historical events. Many of these artworks were commissioned by the government and painted in important buildings in the capital after the Mexican Revolution. Soon, the Mexican muralists' fame spread, and some traveled to cities outside Mexico to paint.

Mexican visual art is still prominent on the

A mural by Diego Rivera fills a wall in the National Palace.

world stage. Perhaps Mexico's most influential contemporary artist is Gabriel Orozco, whose conceptual works in photography, sculpture, drawing, painting, and installation have achieved worldwide acclaim. The preeminent Mexican collector Eugenio López has helped bring attention to contemporary Mexican art.

Mexico also has an extensive tradition of *artesanías*, or handicrafts. This legacy includes an array of beautiful silverwork, intricate embroidery, fanciful and skilled woodcarvings, and a variety of ceramics. Different regions are known for specific crafts. For example, the towns of Dolores Hidalgo in Guanajuato and Puebla in the state of Puebla are known for a type of pottery decorated with floral designs called *talavera*. Metepec, in the state of México, is known for colorful clay suns, while the Seri people of Sonora are recognized for polished wooden carvings. Found throughout the country are the fanciful candelabra-like

TRADITIONAL CLOTHING

People in Mexican cities tend to wear suits and ties, jeans and T-shirts, dresses and high heels— much like people in large cities worldwide. But some wear traditional Mexican clothing for some special occasions and festivals, and this style of dress is favored by some people in rural villages. Women's clothing includes the *huipil*, a long tunic without sleeves worn primarily in southern Mexico; a wraparound skirt called the *enredo* tied with a *faja*, or sash; and a long shawl called a *rebozo*. These garments are made with cotton or wool and embroidered with intricate patterns. Men favor simple pants and shirts with cowboy boots, and they sometimes drape themselves in a blanket-like garment called a *serape*.

handcrafted ceramic figurines collectively called *árbol de la vida*, or "tree of life." Also common are small images painted on tin called *retablos*. These images are left before images of saints in churches and religious sanctuaries to offer thanks for answered prayers.

ARCHITECTURE

Mexican architecture spans thousands of years and embraces some of the world's most unique and elaborate ancient structures, including pyramids and temples from the pre-Hispanic period. Mayan architecture features intricately carved stone surfaces and an innovation called the vault, which is similar to an arch but topped with a capstone. Aztec temples were less detailed but impressive because of their large scale.

Mayan pyramids include materials imported from as far away as Brazil.

Chichén Itzá, located on the Yucatán Peninsula, was declared one of the New Seven Wonders of the World in 2007. Included within this site is the Kukulcán, or "Feathered Serpent" pyramid, which is also known as El Castillo, or "The Castle." The stepped stone structure, a pyramid with steps on the side, measures more than 79 feet (24 m) tall.[1]

During the sixteenth and seventeenth centuries, the primary style for churches and mansions in Mexico was Spanish Gothic, a highly elaborate style with a mixture of decorative elements, or Renaissance, which featured elaborate arches and columns. By the seventeenth

A mariachi band entertains an audience in San Cristóbal de Las Casas in Chiapas.

areas. Most involve colorful costumes, sometimes with elaborate masks, and many are based on Mexico's pre-Hispanic native traditions. Some dances are founded on rituals, and some tell stories. Mexico City's Ballet Folklórico presents a variety of indigenous dances from Mexico.

CHAPTER 7
POLITICS: A TUMULTUOUS DEMOCRACY

Today, Mexico is a vital and thriving democracy. However, its current government was born from a history of colonization, independence, and civil war. After gaining independence from Spain late in the nineteenth century, Mexico endured an invasion from France and withstood a territorial war with the

The current version of the Mexican flag was officially adopted in 1968.

BENITO JUÁREZ

Benito Juárez served five terms as president of Mexico from 1861 to 1872. A Zapotec, he was the first full-blooded indigenous person to serve as the nation's president. He ruled during an era known as *La Reforma,* the Reform, which was named for the social and legislative changes he began.

Benito Pablo Juárez García was born on March 21, 1806, in the village of San Pablo Guelatao in Oaxaca, Mexico. He went to work as a field hand and a shepherd until, at the age of 12, he left his village and walked to the city of Oaxaca to find a better life.

The young Juárez was illiterate and spoke only Zapotec, but he was eager for knowledge. A Franciscan priest was impressed with the young Juárez's intelligence and helped him enter a seminary, a school for priests. Juárez graduated from the seminary in 1827 and went on to earn a law degree from the Instituto de Ciencias y Artes, or the "Institute of Sciences and Arts."

Juárez was a key figure in the reform movement of the 1850s. As president, he secured equal rights for indigenous people, limited the power of the Catholic Church over the Mexican government, and adopted a federal constitution.

United States, eventually ceding much of its northern area to its neighbor.

Mexicans elected their leaders and made use of their democratic powers as early as 1861. In that year, they elected the first indigenous Mexican as president—Benito Juárez, a lawyer, former governor of Oaxaca, and Zapotec Indian. However, the nation's democracy has been challenged over the years by political corruption and calls for fairer elections.

Mexico's tumultuous history explains in part why one political party led the nation from 1920 to 2000. Despite occasional accusations of voter fraud, year after year, the Mexican people elected

The judicial branch is headed by the Supreme Court of Justice. The court consists of 11 judges appointed by the president with approval from the Senate. The judicial branch also includes other judiciary bodies, such as the Electoral Tribunal, which is responsible for resolving disputes that arise within national elections.

Trials decided by juries are not common in Mexico, but Mexican citizens have the right to appeal their cases in a federal court if they are convicted in a local court. The Mexican judiciary has had high caseloads over the years and has weathered accusations of influence by the executive branch. In 1994, the government granted the Supreme Court more independence and more powers of judicial review, which is the ability to declare laws unconstitutional.

Mexico is a democracy with universal suffrage, which means all citizens over age 18 are eligible to vote. Two methods are used to elect officials: plurality and proportional representation. With a plurality system, the candidate with the most votes wins. With proportional representation, representatives are selected according to what percentage of votes each political party receives. For example, a party receiving 30 percent of the votes would receive 30 percent of the 100 seats in the legislature.

Mexican women gained the right to vote in 1947 and the right to run for office in 1953.

The president is elected by plurality for a six-year term and can only serve one term in office. There is no vice president. Congress elects a new president in the event of a president's death or removal from office.

President Felipe Calderón, 2011

Senators serve six-year terms. Ninety-six are elected by plurality, and the rest are elected proportionally according to the votes their political parties received. Of the 500 deputies, 300 are elected by plurality.

been brutally murdered, and kidnappings have been common. In 2009, the city of Juárez, on the border with Texas, became the murder capital of the world, with 2,600 killings, and even more killings occurred in 2010.[5] Although the drug violence is primarily limited to several border cities, it remains a threat to national security and is perhaps the most pressing issue facing the Mexican government today.

CHAPTER 8

ECONOMICS: GROWING TRADE

Mexico has a trillion-dollar economy—the twelfth largest in the world as measured by purchasing power. The nation's per capita gross domestic product (GDP) is $13,800, about one-third that of the United States, ranking it eighty-fifth in the world.[1] Regionally, Mexico has the second-largest economy in Latin America.[2]

In the past decade, Mexico has greatly increased trade with other countries. But despite its growth, the nation still faces severe poverty. President Calderón has made the reduction of poverty and the creation of jobs his top economic priorities.

The Mexican unit of currency is the peso. In 1994, due to a number of factors, including political unrest in Mexico, the peso was severely devalued. It fell from a steady three pesos per one US dollar to four

Many Mexican farmers sell their crops in local markets.

105

THE PESO'S FALLING VALUE

Year	Number of pesos = US$1
2006	10.899
2007	10.8
2008	11.016
2009	13.514
2010	12.687[6]

pesos per dollar.[3] The results sent Mexico into its worst recession in more than half a century.

Throughout the 1990s and into the 2000s, Mexico's economy began recovering, but economic growth was hindered by the world financial crisis in 2008. Mexico's GDP, the total wealth produced by a country, fell by 6.5 percent in 2009. The economy picked up again in 2010, however, growing by 5 percent.[4]

Mexico has a free market economy. This means that buyers and sellers interact based on mutual agreement and with minimal government interference. Mexico has trade agreements with more than 50 countries, including Guatemala, Honduras, El Salvador, European nations, and Japan. These agreements cover more than 90 percent of the nation's trade.[5]

On January 1, 1994, Mexico, the United States, and Canada began following the policies of NAFTA. Designed to make trade easier among the three countries, the agreement eliminated or phased out many of the taxes associated with trade. NAFTA was one of the first such international agreements to include both agriculture and industry and

Mexican pesos are divided into 100 centavos.

NAFTA'S EFFECT ON FARMERS

NAFTA opened up trade among Mexico, the United States, and Canada by reducing the costs of trade and spurring competition and investment. All three nations' economies grew after the implementation of NAFTA, but economists disagree about whether that growth can be attributed to the agreement. Even those in favor of NAFTA agree that its effect on Mexico has been disappointing in relation to the other nations. Mexico's economy has grown, but it has done so more slowly than the economies of the United States and Canada. However, the cost of goods for average Mexicans has decreased dramatically. Mexico's agriculture exports have tripled post-NAFTA, but small farmers continue to struggle to compete against large corporations.

Some economists argue that the growth would have happened with or without the agreement. Alejandro Portes, a sociology professor at Princeton University, stated, "Economic growth has been anemic in Mexico, averaging less than 3.5 percent per year or less than 2 percent on a per capita basis since 2000. . . . Unemployment is higher than what it was when the treaty was signed; and half of the labor force must eke out a living in invented jobs in the informal economy, a figure ten percent higher than in the pre-NAFTA years."[8]

to address environmental issues.

Since implementation of NAFTA, the economies of all three countries have grown, with Canada's economy growing at the fastest rate and Mexico's at the slowest rate. Also since NAFTA, Mexico's trade has greatly increased, and annual exports to the United States have more than quadrupled, from $60 billion to $280 billion per year.[7] However, economists debate the effects of NAFTA, and some argue that it has worsened the economic situation for Mexico's rural population and small farmers.

Many Mexicans work in the manufacturing industry.

IMPORTS AND EXPORTS

Mexico is rich in natural resources, including petroleum, silver, copper, gold, lead, zinc, natural gas, and timber. Currently, the nation is undergoing a transition to a service economy, and services make up 62.5 percent of the GDP. Industries bring in 33.3 percent, and agriculture contributes only 4.2 percent to the GDP.[9]

Mexico's primary industries are oil and manufacturing, including tobacco, chemicals, mining, textiles, clothing, motor vehicles, consumer goods, food and beverages, and iron and steel. Tourism is the third-largest industry in Mexico.

Evidence suggests that corn was first cultivated in Mexico.

Although agriculture makes up only a small percentage of the GDP, 13.7 percent of the population work in agricultural jobs.[10] Mexican farmers cultivate corn, wheat, soybeans, rice, beans, cotton, coffee, fruit, tomatoes, beef, poultry, dairy products, and wood products.

Mexico exports manufactured goods, silver, fruits, vegetables, coffee, cotton, and oil and petroleum products. Its imports include metalworking machines, steel mill products, agricultural machinery, electric equipment, car parts for assembly, repair parts for motor vehicles, aircraft, and aircraft parts.

Mexico's chief trading partner is the United States, which purchases a large majority of Mexico's exports. Other significant partners are Canada, Germany, China, and Japan. The United States buys 80.5 percent of Mexican exports, Canada buys 3.6 percent, and Germany buys 1.4 percent. Mexico buys 48 percent of its imports from the United States, 13.5 percent from China, and 4.8 percent from Japan.[11]

CURRENT OUTLOOK

One of Mexico's key economic goals is to close the big gap that exists between its rich and poor people. Mexico is faced with the challenges of

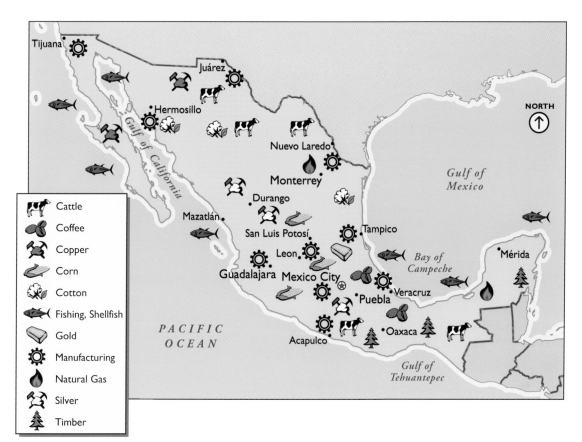

Cattle
Coffee
Copper
Corn
Cotton
Fishing, Shellfish
Gold
Manufacturing
Natural Gas
Silver
Timber

Resources of Mexico

growing its middle class and creating more jobs, particularly for its many citizens who go to the United States to work.

An example of this economic problem can be found in an area of Mexico City called Santa Fe. In the late 1980s, developers transformed

MEXICAN REMITTANCES

The Mexican economy depends in part on the money sent home by Mexicans who have left the country to work abroad. Many of these workers immigrate to the United States. The amounts of money workers send home are called remittances, and each year, Mexicans living in the United States send billions of dollars in remittances to their families in Mexico.

In recent years, the global recession has made it more difficult for many people to make a living, and remittances have decreased. In 2007, Mexicans sent $26 billion dollars to their families in Mexico. In 2008, they sent $25 billion. This was the first time in at least 13 years the amount of yearly remittances had declined.[14]

the area into a hub for international business, constructing modern office buildings and expensive condominiums. Only a mile or two from this refurbished area is the part of the city called *el pueblo*. There, 240,000 residents live in bunker-like homes covered with plastic roofs and clinging in clusters to crowded hillsides.[12] Mexico is home to large multinational corporations and some of the world's richest people, yet it also has widespread poverty.

A 2004 United Nations report showed that people in some rural regions of southern Mexico lived in conditions similar to those in the poorest areas of Africa, whereas the standard of living in other Mexican communities was similar to that of wealthy areas of Spain and Germany.[13] Poverty and hunger are particularly widespread in rural Mexico. A report by the Confederación Nacional Campesina (CNC), or the "National Peasant Confederation,"

Larger cities in Mexico have thriving business centers, similar to the stock exchange in Mexico City.

Mexico works to decrease the numbers of people living in poverty, but it is still a problem in both urban and rural environments.

found that 70 percent of indigenous children in Mexico do not have enough food to eat.[15]

But poverty is not limited to rural areas. A government report found that one in five Mexican families in metropolitan areas were living in poverty, due in large part to lack of adequate jobs and economic opportunities.[16] When poverty is defined by having enough money for food, 18.2 percent of Mexicans live below the poverty line. When poverty is defined by assets, however, 47 percent live below the poverty line.[17]

Other economic challenges include improving the education system, modernizing labor laws, and promoting private investment in energy.

Mexico's economy has depended heavily on oil for many years, but recently, the nation has become less dependent on this natural resource.

Mexico has decreased poverty to some extent and improved access to education. The nation's economic outlook is improving, but opening up economic opportunities to more of its citizens remains a key challenge. Evidence of this can be found in the vast number of citizens working in what is called the informal economy: people who earn a living outside the bounds of registered jobs. As a result of the depressed global economy, the numbers of Mexicans entering the informal economy increased from 28.1 to 28.8 percent in 2009.[18] Many set up stalls or makeshift booths on streets, selling items such as handicrafts, foods, electronics, books, and more. Others worked as street musicians or in other performances, and still others cooked, cleaned, or performed various services in unofficial capacities, earning whatever they could to make a living.

PEMEX

Mexico is a major producer and exporter of oil, and the industry brings in approximately one-third of the government's revenue each year.[19] Because of this, personal income taxes and business taxes are much lower in Mexico than in other countries. In 1938, the government nationalized the industry, creating a company called Pemex as the single oil company in the nation. Pemex is Mexico's largest company and one of the world's biggest oil and natural gas companies.[20]

CHAPTER 9
MEXICO TODAY

Similar to people in most countries, Mexicans are a diverse group, and every region, community, family, and individual has unique characteristics. One common link among most Mexicans, however, is the importance of family. In addition, Mexicans tend to identify with their local community and to have strong ties to their home village, city, state, or region and to the nation as a whole.

Mexican people tend to be tolerant, hardworking, and generous. Religion, the arts, and time spent with friends and family are key elements of their lives. Mexican people work hard and have a strong work ethic, but the pace of life is less hectic than it is in other developed parts of the world, including the United States. Even in big cities, Mexicans are not afraid to take time for leisurely lunches, and their workday does not start until 10:00 a.m. But with new industries, shopping centers, and other activities, the leisurely pace of the workday is changing rapidly for many Mexicans.

Spending time with family is an important part of Mexican life.

For the most part, men are considered to be the head of the family in Mexico. A culture of machismo—an exaggerated masculine attitude—has predominated in Mexico for a long time. However, this attitude has lessened significantly over the decades. Migration of men to cities and to the United States has dramatically increased the number of female-headed households, especially in rural areas.

Although Mexico is primarily a Catholic country, a religion that opposes abortion, the Mexican government upheld legalized abortion, giving women the right to choose in cases of an unwanted pregnancy. Notably, the nation also has a relatively liberal policy toward gays and lesbians. In 2010, Mexico's supreme court recognized the right of same-sex couples to adopt children in Mexico City.

"Mexico City is poised to be a vanguard of [the twenty-first century]. Culturally, economically, and politically, it can be seen as the capital of the Spanish-speaking world."[2]

—David Lida, journalist and author of First Stop in the New World: Mexico City, The Capital of the 21st Century

EDUCATION IN MEXICO

Mexico has a free public education system, and Mexican children attend school for 14 years on average.[1] Attendance in primary school, first through sixth grade, has been required since the 1917 constitution. The required number of years was increased in 1992 to include lower secondary school, which is up to ninth grade. Most students attend pre-primary school, six years of elementary school, three years of junior high school, and three years of preparatory school, or high school.

Since the 1950s, enrollment in education has increased dramatically. From 1950 to 2000, the number of students enrolled in education, from primary school through graduate school, increased from 3.25 million to 28.22 million.[3] In 1970, only 9 percent of the population of Mexico was educated up to the ninth grade, but by 1998, this level had increased to 41.4 percent.[4]

STUDENT ENROLLMENT IN MEXICO (2008)

Pre-Primary	Primary (grades 1–6)	Secondary (grades 7–13, includes junior high and high school)	Tertiary (college or technical school)
100 percent	98 percent	74 percent (girls) 71 percent (boys)	27 percent[5]

This growth in education has fueled learning but also put pressure on schools. Until 1992, the federal government controlled Mexican

education. The centralized system had a national curriculum and held all schools to the same requirements. Critics saw the curriculum as too rigid, limiting creativity and critical thinking. In 1993, the majority of control over education was placed in the hands of the state governments. Some states began school reform, but critics maintain that Mexican schools still emphasize memorization over creativity.

Other challenges to education in Mexico include overcrowding in schools, limited funds, and inequity between the wealthy and the poor. The large number of students makes it difficult to have adequate facilities, and many classrooms are crowded. Although the Mexican government has placed a priority on education, the budget for schools is not sufficient to build facilities at the pace of enrollment.

The literacy rate in Mexico is 86.1 percent.[6] Literacy has increased significantly in recent years as a result of the government's emphasis on improving access to education. Even so, the rate of literacy varies from region to region. In poverty-stricken and rural areas, it remains a challenge to get children to attend school regularly and to stay in school long enough to learn to read and write.

> There are 83.5 million cell phones in use in Mexico, the thirteenth most in the world.

Children at school in a rural Mexican village

SWEET FIFTEEN

Throughout Mexico, adolescent girls look forward to their fifteenth birthday with eager anticipation. An elaborate and festive celebration called a *quinceañera* (*quince* means "fifteen" in Spanish) marks a girl's transition into womanhood.

The quinceañera is a special event, and girls dress accordingly. They typically don long, frilly dresses, not unlike wedding gowns, and often wear matching hats or headpieces. The birthday girl is accompanied by attendants—young men and women invited to assist or chaperone for the day—as well as her parents and godparents.

In this predominantly Catholic country, the quinceañera begins in church, where the teen is seated at the altar along with her party of attendants and sponsors. The church ceremony is traditionally followed by a big party. Friends and family members celebrate with feasting and dancing and enjoy a large, decorative cake.

Hosting a quinceañera is very involved and tends to be costly. Families often save for years for a daughter's quinceañera. Some ask sponsors, in addition to the godparents, to participate; for example, one might purchase the dress and another the cake. This way, families and communities come together in celebrating the young woman's coming of age.

MEXICAN TEENS

As a whole, Mexican teens value education and have a deep respect for their teachers. They have often been taught since they were young that having an education is the key to their future, and they aim to work hard and earn a good education. At the same time, many Mexican teens struggle with issues that make it difficult to stay in school. One or both parents may work outside the country—a stressful situation for teens. Local drug-related violence is another stressor many teens face on a daily basis. In addition, teens living in or near poverty-stricken areas feel a deep responsibility to help their families and must often work after school or

Teens perform in a musical ensemble.

drop out to help with the household economy. Most teens in Mexico also spend time helping out at home, cooking, cleaning, or caring for younger siblings.

Although many Mexican teens work hard at school and a job, they enjoy the same kinds of activities as adolescents in other areas of the world. They listen to music, spend time with friends, eat meals with their families, use the Internet, and participate in their communities. Mexican teens in cities have access to museums, movie theaters, and more, similar to teens in most cities around the world. For teens in rural villages, the pace of life tends to be slower. Plazas throughout Mexico provide places to visit with friends.

The Cinco de Mayo holiday is more widely celebrated in the United States than in Mexico.

FUTURE OUTLOOK

Based on Mexico's past, its future is certain to be fascinating, and its unique culture is likely to thrive. Mexican cuisine is already known throughout North America and beyond. And as more and more Mexican artists, musicians, and entertainers extend their talents to the world stage, Mexican culture will be even more widely recognized and influential than it is today.

Mexico's primary current challenge is its fight against the drug cartels. Drug lords rule over some cities, terrorizing anyone who gets in the way of the illegal international drug trade, including local and federal police. Whether the government can succeed in battling the powerful and violent drug trade will have a significant effect on Mexico's future.

Tourism continues to be an important industry in Mexico, as people come from all over the world to enjoy the natural beauty of the nation's

beaches and deserts and the architectural relics of its glorious past. Drug-related violence has kept some tourists away, but because the violence occurs in isolated areas of the country, continued education and awareness about the nature of the problem will help persuade tourists to visit.

Environmental problems also continue to plague Mexico, but efforts at protecting the country's rich and varied resources are having positive effects. Adventure companies offering ecotourism help the country maintain its ecology and continue to draw tourists. Mexico is also positioning itself to become a leader in sustainable energy, including solar power.

SOLAR ENERGY PROGRAM

In a world where renewable energy is becoming increasingly important, Mexico has begun accessing its sunny climate and natural water resources to create renewable energy. One-sixth of the nation's energy comes from hydroelectric dams.[7] Mexico is actively seeking foreign investment to continue to develop solar power.

Mexico's relationship with the United States and Canada can help the country continue to grow economically. The middle class is growing and the outlook is positive that this growth will continue to surge ahead in the future, creating a more balanced economy for the citizens of this vibrant nation.

Despite the challenges that face Mexico, its people continue to work hard and to be proud of their rich culture.

TIMELINE

30,000–12,000 BCE	The first people come to the land that is now Mexico, crossing over the Bering Strait, a land bridge from Asia.
1200–400 BCE	The Olmec civilization thrives along the Gulf coast in the south of Mexico.
250–900 CE	The Mayan civilization thrives in southwest Mexico and parts of Central America.
700–1200	The Toltec civilization begins and flourishes.
1325–1521	The Aztec civilization settles in central Mexico in the city of Tenochtitlán and develops a sophisticated and hierarchical society.
1519	Spanish ships led by Hernán Cortés arrive in Mexico and topple the Aztec regime by 1521.
1810	Mexico's wars of independence begin on September 16.
1821	Mexico achieves independence from Spain.
1824	Mexico's first constitution establishes the government as a federal republic.
1836	On March 6, Mexican forces enter Texas and win the Battle of the Alamo.
1846–1848	The Mexican-American War is fought; the United States takes territories from Mexico.
1861	Benito Juárez, a Zapotec attorney and reformist political leader, becomes Mexico's first fully indigenous president.

1863–1867	France invades Mexico and controls Mexico City.
1876–1911	Porfirio Díaz is president of Mexico and rules the country as a dictatorship.
1910–1911	Mexicans revolt against Díaz, and he resigns in May 1911.
1911–1920	One in eight Mexicans are killed in the Mexican Revolution.
1929	The National Revolutionary Party (PRI) begins and controls Mexico until 2000.
1938	The Mexican government forms Pemex, the national oil company.
1970s	World oil prices rise and the Mexican economy benefits, selling oil through Pemex.
1980s	Oil prices fall, causing a widespread economic recession throughout Mexico.
1994	The North American Free Trade Agreement (NAFTA) takes effect, opening up more trade among Mexico, the United States, and Canada.
2000	Vicente Fox wins the presidency of Mexico for the National Action Party (PAN).
2006	Felipe Calderón wins an initially disputed election for the presidency against Andrés Manuel López Obrador.
2010	More than 12,400 people die as a result of drug trafficking.

FACTS AT YOUR FINGERTIPS

GEOGRAPHY

Official name: United Mexican States (in Spanish, Estados Unidos Mexicanos)

Area: 758,304,639 square miles (1,964,375 sq km)

Climate: Sunny with a mostly temperate climate, although the weather varies in different regions. It is hot and humid along the coasts, particularly in the south, from May through September. The central and northern regions get chilly from November through February. Most parts of the country are rainy from June through October.

Highest elevation: Volcán Pico de Orizaba, 18,700 feet (5,700 m) above sea level

Lowest elevation: Laguna Salada, 33 feet (10 m) below sea level

Significant geographic features: Pico de Orizaba and Iztaccíhuatl, volcanoes

PEOPLE

Population (July 2011 est.): 113,724,226

Most populous city: Mexico City

Ethnic groups: mestizo, 60 percent; Amerindian or predominantly

Amerindian, 30 percent; white, 9 percent; other, 1 percent

Percentage of residents living in urban areas: 78 percent

Life expectancy: 76.47 years at birth (world rank: 73)

Language(s): Spanish only, 92.7 percent; Spanish and indigenous languages (includes Mayan, Nahuatl, and other regional languages), 5.7 percent; indigenous only, 0.8 percent; unspecified, 0.8 percent

Religion(s): Roman Catholicism, 76.5 percent; Protestantism, 6.3 percent; other, 0.3 percent; unspecified, 13.8 percent; none, 3.1 percent

GOVERNMENT AND ECONOMY

Government: federal republic

Capital: Mexico City

Date of adoption of current constitution: February 5, 1917

Head of state and head of government: president

Legislature: National Congress, consists of the Senate and the Chamber of Deputies

Currency: peso

Industries and natural resources: manufacturing, tourism, petroleum, silver, copper, gold, lead, zinc, natural gas, timber

NATIONAL SYMBOLS

Holidays: September 16, Independence Day, is a national holiday commemorating the day in 1810 that Mexico declared independence from Spain.

Flag: Three equally sized vertical bands of green, white, and red. In the center white band is an image of an eagle on a cactus with a snake.

National anthem: "Himno Nacional Mexicano" ("National Anthem of Mexico"), used since 1854 but adopted officially in 1943.

National animal: golden eagle

KEY PEOPLE

Montezuma, the last emperor of the Aztecs

Benito Juárez, president of Mexico from 1861 until his death in 1872

Pancho Villa, Mexican folk hero, began as a Robin Hood–like bandit, defending the poor, and later emerged as a leader of the Mexican Revolution

STATES OF MEXICO

State; Capital

Aguascalientes; Aguascalientes

Baja California; Mexicali

Baja California Sur; La Paz

Campeche; Campeche

Chiapas; Tuxtla Gutiérrez

Chihuahua; Chihuahua

Coahuila; Saltillo

Colima; Colima

* Distrito Federal; Ciudad de México

Durango; Durango

Guanajuato; Guanajuato

Guerrero; Chilpancingo

Hidalgo; Pachuca

Jalisco; Guadalajara

México; Toluca

Michoacán; Morelia

Morelos; Cuernavaca

Nayarit; Tepic

Nuevo León; Monterrey

Oaxaca; Oaxaca

Puebla; Puebla

Querétaro; Querétaro

Quintana Roo; Chetumal

San Luis Potosí; San Luis Potosí

Sinaloa; Culiacán

Sonora; Hermosillo

Tabasco; Villahermosa

Tamaulipas; Ciudad Victoria

Tlaxcala; Tlaxcala

Veracruz; Xalapa

Yucatán; Mérida

Zacatecas; Zacatecas

* Mexico's federal district

GLOSSARY

altiplano
A plateau; the central region of Mexico between the Sierra Mountains.

Amerindian
Of American Indian descent; indigenous to America.

annex
To incorporate an area or territory into an existing one.

biodiversity
The variety of plant and animal life in a particular habitat.

biosphere
Living organisms, plants and animals, and the natural environment they inhabit.

cartel
An organization or business organized to control the production, distribution, and price of a given product, such as drugs.

conquistadores
Spanish word for *conquerors*; used to describe the Spaniards that conquered the Aztecs.

criollos
People of Spanish descent at the top of the hierarchical social structure of Spanish America.

hierarchy
A classification of people by a given quality or trait—usually by race, ability, or economic or professional status.

indigenous

Originally or naturally belonging to an area.

Mesoamerica

An anthropological term used to describe the area from central Mexico to northern Honduras in which pre-Hispanic civilizations flourished.

mestizo

An ethnicity that describes a person of mixed Amerindian, European, and sometimes African ancestry.

mural

A large wall painting, usually in a public place.

pre-Hispanic

The time period before the Spanish conquest of Mexico.

ADDITIONAL RESOURCES

SELECTED BIBLIOGRAPHY

Lida, David. *First Stop in the New World: Mexico City, The Capital of the 21st Century.* New York: Riverhead, 2008. Print.

Merrill, Tim L., and Ramón Miró. *Mexico: A Country Study.* Washington DC: Government Printing Office, 1996. Print and Web.

Noble, John. *Lonely Planet Mexico.* Oakland, CA: Lonely Planet, 2010. Print.

FURTHER READINGS

Berne, Emma Carlson. *Frida Kahlo: Mexican Artist.* Edina, MN: ABDO, 2009. Print.

Grabman, Richard. *Gods, Gachupines and Gringos: A People's History of Mexico.* Albuquerque, NM: Editorial Mazatlán, 2008. Print.

Phillips, Charles. *The Everyday Life of the Aztec & Maya.* London, UK: Southwater, 2007. Print.

WEB LINKS

To learn more about Mexico, visit ABDO Publishing Company online at **www.abdopublishing.com**. Web sites about Mexico are featured on our Book Links page. These links are routinely monitored and updated to provide the most current information available.

PLACES TO VISIT

If you are ever in Mexico, consider checking out these important and interesting sites!

Chichén Itzá

This temple and pyramid complex is located on the Yucatán Peninsula of Mexico.

Land's End, Cabo San Lucas, Baja California

Visit El Arco (The Arch), a rocky arc rising out of the blue water at the tip of the Baja Peninsula, home to pelicans, sea lions, and dazzling sunsets.

Museo Nacional de Antropología (National Archaeological Museum)

This famous museum is located in Chapultepec Park in Mexico City and is a great place to view relics from Mexico's amazing early civilizations.

SOURCE NOTES

CHAPTER 1. A VISIT TO MEXICO

1. John Noble. *Lonely Planet Mexico.* Oakland, CA: Lonely Planet, 2010. Print. 122.

2. Ibid. 98.

3. "Juarez's Birthday: Mexico and Its Culture." *Presidency of the Republic of Mexico.* Presidency of the Republic of Mexico, n.d. Web. 10 Feb. 2011.

4. "The World Factbook: Mexico." *Central Intelligence Agency.* Central Intelligence Agency, 20 Jan. 2011. Web. 10 Feb. 2011.

5. Ibid.

CHAPTER 2. GEOGRAPHY: A RICH AND VARIED LANDSCAPE

1. "The World Factbook: Mexico." *Central Intelligence Agency.* Central Intelligence Agency, 20 Jan. 2011. Web. 10 Feb. 2011.

2. Ibid.

3. John Noble. *Lonely Planet Mexico.* Oakland, CA: Lonely Planet, 2010. Print. 89.

4. Ibid.

5. "Rio Grande." *Encyclopædia Britannica.* Encyclopædia Britannica, 2011. Web. 10 Feb. 2011.

6. "Lake Chapala." *Encyclopædia Britannica.* Encyclopædia Britannica, 2011. Web. 10 Feb. 2011.

7. Tim L. Merrill, and Ramón Miró. *Mexico: A Country Study.* Washington DC: Government Printing Office, 1996. Web. 10 Feb. 2011.

8. "On This Day: September 19, 1985." *BBC.* BBC, 2011. Web. 10 Feb. 2011.

9. Tim L. Merrill, and Ramón Miró. *Mexico: A Country Study.* Washington DC: Government Printing Office, 1996. Web. 10 Feb. 2011.

10. "Country Guide: Mexico." *BBC: Weather.* BBC, n.d. Web. 14 Jan. 2011.

CHAPTER 3. ANIMALS AND NATURE: DIVERSITY FROM LAND TO SEA

1. Santiago Enriquez. "Assessment of Tropical Forest and Biodiversity Conservation in Mexico." *USAID.* United States Agency of International Development, 2007. Web. 13 Feb. 2011.

2. "Fauna of Mexico—Birds (Aves)." *Viva Natura.org.* VN, 2003. Web. 10 Feb. 2011.

3. Santiago Enriquez. "Assessment of Tropical Forest and Biodiversity Conservation in Mexico." *USAID.* United States Agency of International Development, 2007. Web. 13 Feb. 2011.

4. "Plants of Mexico." *Viva Natura.org.* VN, 2003. Web. 10 Feb. 2011.

5. "Vaquita: Phocoena sinus." *Project Global.* Nicholas School of the Environment and Earth Sciences at Duke University, n.d. Web. 10 Feb. 2011.

6. "Phocoena sinus." *IUCN Red List of Threatened Species.* International Union for Conservation of Nature and Natural Resources, 2010. Web. 6 Apr. 2011.

7. John Noble. *Lonely Planet Mexico.* Oakland, CA: Lonely Planet, 2010. Print. 91.

8. Santiago Enriquez. "Assessment of Tropical Forest and Biodiversity Conservation in Mexico." *USAID.* United States Agency of International Development, 2007. Web. 13 Feb. 2011.

9. John Noble. *Lonely Planet Mexico.* Oakland, CA: Lonely Planet, 2010. Print. 91.

10. Ibid. 93.

11. Ibid. 91.

12. "Summary Statistics: Summaries by Country, Table 5, Threatened Species in Each Country." *IUCN Red List of Threatened Species.* International Union for Conservation of Nature and Natural Resources, 2010. Web. 13 Feb. 2011.

13. Ibid.

CHAPTER 4. HISTORY: AN EPIC PAST

1. John Noble. *Lonely Planet Mexico.* Oakland, CA: Lonely Planet, 2010. Print. 41.

2. Tim L. Merrill, and Ramón Miró. *Mexico: A Country Study.* Washington DC: Government Printing Office, 1996. Web. 10 Feb. 2011.

3. John Noble. *Lonely Planet Mexico.* Oakland, CA: Lonely Planet, 2010. Print. 45.

4. Ibid.

CHAPTER 5. PEOPLE: A PROUD NATION

1. "The World Factbook: Mexico." *Central Intelligence Agency.* Central Intelligence Agency, 20 Jan. 2011. Web. 10 Feb. 2011.

2. John Noble. *Lonely Planet Mexico.* Oakland, CA: Lonely Planet, 2010. Print. 59.

3. "The World Factbook: Mexico." *Central Intelligence Agency.* Central Intelligence Agency, 20 Jan. 2011. Web. 10 Feb. 2011.

4. Ibid.

5. Ibid.

6. John Noble. *Lonely Planet Mexico.* Oakland, CA: Lonely Planet, 2010. Print. 58.

7. "The World Factbook: Mexico." *Central Intelligence Agency.* Central Intelligence Agency, 20 Jan. 2011. Web. 10 Feb. 2011.

8. Ibid.

9. Ibid.

10. "The Largest Catholic Communities." *Adherants.com.* Adherants.com, n.d. Web. 10 Feb. 2011.

SOURCE NOTES CONTINUED

11. Carolyn Lochhead. "Give and Take Across the Border." *SF Gate*. Hearst Communications, 21 Mar. 2006. Web. 10 Feb. 2011.

12. Ibid.

CHAPTER 6. CULTURE: VIBRANT AND UNIQUE

1. "El Castillo." *Encyclopædia Britannica*. Encyclopædia Britannica, 2011. Web. 10 Feb. 2011.

2. John Noble. *Lonely Planet Mexico*. Oakland, CA: Lonely Planet, 2010. Print. 71.

CHAPTER 7. POLITICS: A TUMULTUOUS DEMOCRACY

1. John Noble. *Lonely Planet Mexico*. Oakland, CA: Lonely Planet, 2010. Print. 49.

2. Agencia Pulsar. "Mexico: Most Violent Year for Calderón." *Argentina Independent*. Argentina Independent, 7 Jan. 2011. Web. 10 Feb. 2011.

3. Ibid.

4. Associated Press. "Mexico: Drug War Toll Tops 30,000." *New York Times*. New York Times, 16 Dec. 2010. Web. 10 Feb. 2011.

5. Barry Petersen. "Juarez, Mexico—Murder Capital of the World." *CBS Evening News*. CBS News, 12 Aug. 2010. Web. 10 Feb. 2011.

CHAPTER 8. ECONOMICS: GROWING TRADE

1. "The World Factbook: Mexico." *Central Intelligence Agency*. Central Intelligence Agency, 20 Jan. 2011. Web. 10 Feb. 2011.

2. "Mexico Country Profile." *BBC News*. BBC, 29 Nov. 2010. Web. 10 Feb. 2011.

3. Joachim Zietz. "Why Did the Peso Collapse? Implications for American Trade." *Global Commerce*, Summer 1995: Volume 1, Number 1.

4. "The World Factbook: Mexico." *Central Intelligence Agency*. Central Intelligence Agency, 20 Jan. 2011. Web. 10 Feb. 2011.

5. Ibid.

6. Ibid.

7. Lee Hudson Teslik. "NAFTA's Economic Impact." *Council on Foreign Relations*. Council on Foreign Relations, 7 Jul. 2009. Web. 10 Feb. 2011.

8. Ibid.

9. "The World Factbook: Mexico." *Central Intelligence Agency*. Central Intelligence Agency, 20 Jan. 2011. Web. 10 Feb. 2011.

10. Ibid.

11. Ibid.

12. David Lida. *First Stop in the New World: Mexico City, The Capital of the 21ˢᵗ Century*. New York: Riverhead, 2008. Print. 51.

13. SourceMex Economic News & Analysis on Mexico. "Report Signs Spotlight on Continuing Poverty in Mexico." *AllBusiness.com*. AllBusiness.com, 27 Oct. 2004. Web. 10 Feb. 2011.

14. Sara Miller Llana. "Mexican Workers Send Less Cash Home from the US." *Christian Science Monitor*. Christian Science Monitor, 28 Jan. 2009. Web. 10 Feb. 2011.

15. SourceMex Economic News & Analysis on Mexico. "Report Signs Spotlight on Continuing Poverty in Mexico." *AllBusiness.com*. AllBusiness.com, 27 Oct. 2004. Web. 10 Feb. 2011.

16. Ibid.

17. "The World Factbook: Mexico." *Central Intelligence Agency*. Central Intelligence Agency, 20 Jan. 2011. Web. 10 Feb. 2011.

18. Caroline Stauffer, and Patrick Rucker. "Mexico's Informal Economy Swells through Recovery." *Reuters*. Reuters, 25 Aug. 2010. Web. 10 Feb. 2011.

19. "Mexico Country Profile." *BBC News*. BBC, 29 Nov. 2010. Web. 10 Feb. 2011.

20. "Mexico: Oil." *US Energy Information Administration*. US Department of Energy, June 2010. Web. 10 Feb. 2011. http://www.eia.doe.gov/cabs/Mexico/Oil.html

CHAPTER 9. MEXICO TODAY

1. "The World Factbook: Mexico." *Central Intelligence Agency*. Central Intelligence Agency, 20 Jan. 2011. Web. 10 Feb. 2011.

2. David Lida. *First Stop in the New World: Mexico City, The Capital of the 21ˢᵗ Century*. New York: Riverhead, 2008. Print. 326.

3. Kevin Rowling. "Education in Mexico." *WENR World Education News and Reviews*. World Education Services, June 2006. Web. 10 Feb. 2011.

4. Ibid.

5. "UIS Statistics in Brief: Education in Mexico." *UNESCO Institute for Statistics*. UNESCO Institute for Statistics, 2008. Web. 10 Feb. 2011.

6. "The World Factbook: Mexico." *Central Intelligence Agency*. Central Intelligence Agency, 20 Jan. 2011. Web. 10 Feb. 2011.

7. John Noble. *Lonely Planet Mexico*. Oakland, CA: Lonely Planet, 2010. Print. 93.

INDEX

Acapulco, 30
animals, 15, 33–35, 38–39, 41–42, 50
architecture, 73, 79, 83–85
art, 8, 14, 15, 16, 46, 48, 61, 73, 79–83, 85, 117, 124
Aztec, 8–10, 49–52, 62, 67, 69, 74, 79, 83, 86, 99

Baja California, 21, 35–36, 79
Baja Peninsula, 26, 28
Belize, 23, 46, 48
bordering countries, 18, 21–23

Cabo San Lucas, 26
Calderón, Felipe, 58–59, 94, 99, 101, 105
California, Gulf of, 21, 35
Calles, Plutarco Elías, 57–58
Canada, 39, 63, 101, 106, 108, 110, 126
Cancún, 26
Caribbean Sea, 21, 24
Chapala, Lake, 26
Chapultepec Park, 14
Chihuahuan Desert, 36
China, 65, 74, 110
climate, 21, 26, 126
constitution, 53–54, 92, 95, 119,
Cordillera Neo–Volcánica, 23
Cortés, Hernán, 50
currency, 19, 105–106

del Toro, Guillermo, 87
Díaz, Porfirio, 56, 91
drug cartels, 101–103, 124–125

economic growth, 58, 106–108
education, 54, 65, 114–115, 118–121, 122, 125
El Salvador, 48, 106
endangered species, 35, 41–42
environmental threats, 38–39, 41, 108, 125
Esquivel, Laura, 85
exports, 108, 109–111, 115

food, 12, 36, 49, 75–77, 109, 114, 115
Fox, Vicente, 58, 94, 100
Fuentes, Carlos, 85

García Bernal, Gael, 87
government structure, 19, 95–99
gross domestic product, 18, 19, 105, 106, 109, 110
Guadalajara, 28, 77
Guanajuato, 23, 53, 80, 82, 94
Guatemala, 23, 24, 46, 48, 106
Guaymas, 30
Guzmán, Alejandra, 88

Hidalgo, Miguel, 8, 53, 82
holidays, 69, 73, 91
Honduras, 46, 48, 106

imports, 67, 109–110
independence, 7–8, 12, 53–59, 67, 91, 100
industries, 108, 109–110, 115, 117, 125
infrastructure, 71
Institutional Revolutionary Party, 57–58, 93, 94, 99

Juárez, 23, 103
Juárez, Benito, 54–55, 92

Kahlo, Frida, 14, 80

language, 10, 19, 61, 64–65, 85
leaders, current, 94, 99
Legorreta, Ricardo, 85
Lerma River, 26
life expectancy, 67
literacy rate, 121
literature, 73, 85–87
López Obrador, Andrés Manuel, 94

Maya, 48–50, 62, 65, 74, 79, 83
Mérida, 23
Mexican Army, 7
Mexico, Gulf of, 21, 23, 24, 26, 28, 41–42

Mexico City, 7, 10, 12, 14–15, 16, 19, 23, 28, 30, 47, 49, 55, 58, 73, 77, 85, 89, 94, 99, 111, 118
Monterrey, 30, 76
music, 15, 16, 73, 88–89, 115, 124

Nahuatl, 10, 15, 65
National Action Party, 58, 99
National Anthropological Museum, 15, 85
national capital, 16, 18, 19, 23, 28, 58
National Palace, 8
national parks, 39
natural resources, 40, 52, 109

Oaxaca, 62, 76, 92
Obregón, Álvaro, 56
official name, 19
Olmec, 46, 48, 79
Orozco, Gabriel, 82

Pacheco, José Emilio, 85
Pacific Ocean, 21, 23
Partido Revolucionario Institucional, 57, 58, 93, 94, 99
Paseo de la Reforma, 12, 14
Paz, Octavio, 85, 86
plants, 33, 34, 35–39, 42, 45, 69, 75
political parties, 98–99

Poniatowska, Elena, 85
population, 19, 52, 53, 58, 65, 67, 68, 69, 108, 110, 119
Portal de Mercaderes, 8
poverty, 18, 105, 112–115, 121, 122
Puebla, 62, 76, 82
Puerto Vallarta, 26

religion, 19, 46, 53, 61, 67–69, 117, 118
Rio Grande, 26, 54
Rivera, Diego, 8, 80
Rubio, Paulina, 88

Sierra Madre del Sur, 24
Sierra Madre Occidental, 23
Sierra Madre Oriental, 23
Siqueiros, David Alfaro, 80
Sonoran Desert, 26, 36
Spain, 8, 52, 61, 86, 91, 112
sports, 77–79

Tamayo, Rufino, 80
teenage life, 122–124
Tehuantepec, Isthmus of, 24
Templo Mayor, 10, 49
Tenochtitlán, 10, 49, 52
Teotihuacán, 47, 99
tourism, 26, 110, 125, 126

United Nations Educational, Scientific, and Cultural Organization World Heritage sites, 10, 39
United States, 18, 21, 26, 42, 54, 63, 69–71, 79, 86, 92, 100–101, 105, 106, 108, 110, 111, 112, 117, 118, 126

Vázquez, Pedro Ramírez, 85
Victoria, Guadalupe, 53
Volcano of Fire, 24

Yucatán Peninsula, 24, 26, 48, 62, 77, 83

PHOTO CREDITS

Alex Garaev/Fotolia, cover; iStockphoto, 2, 68, 89, 96, 113; Stephen Meese/Shutterstock Images, 5 (top), 43; Elena Fernandez Zabelguelskaya/Shutterstock Images, 5 (middle), 44, 128 (top); Rui Vale de Sousa/Shutterstock Images, 5 (bottom), 125; Dallas and John Heaton/Photolibrary, 6; Bigstock, 9; Matt Kania/Map Hero, Inc., 11, 27, 29, 63, 111; Robert Maxwell/iStockphoto, 13; Schildge Bill/Photolibrary, 17; Andrew Howard/Shutterstock Images, 20; Marco Regalia/Shutterstock Images, 22; Carrie Winegarden/iStockphoto, 25; Xavier Arnau/iStockphoto, 31; Natalie-Claude Bélanger/iStockphoto, 32; David Schrader/iStockphoto, 34; Elisabeth Eaves/iStockphoto, 37; Miguel Malo/iStockphoto, 40; Kate Connes/Shutterstock Images, 47; Time & Life Pictures/Getty Images, 51, 57, 128 (bottom); AFP/Getty Images, 55; David de la Paz/AP Images, 59; Walter Bibikow/Photolibrary, 60; Andres Balcazar/iStockphoto, 66, 130; Alan Diaz/AP Images, 71; Shutterstock Images, 72, 75, 84, 90, 132, 107, 131, 127; Eduardo Verdugo/AP Images, 78; Ron Giling/Photolibrary, 81; Miguel Tovar/AP Images, 93; Evan Vucci/AP Images, 98, 129; Alexandre Meneghini/AP Images, 102; Hauke Dressler/LOOK-foto/Photolibrary, 104; Danny Lehman/Photolibrary, 109; Milan Klusacek/iStockphoto, 114; Aldo Murillo/iStockphoto, 116; Mark Edwards/Photolibrary, 120; Michael Snell/Photolibrary, 123